SANJA KON

WEB3 and BLOCKCHAIN 4 WOMEN

A GUIDE FOR WOMEN ON WORKING, INVESTING AND THRIVING IN THE BITCOIN ECONOMY

Preface of Peter Diamandis

*To my precious son Noah,
as you embark on life's journey,
know that my greatest wish
for you is to follow your dreams
and achieve greatness.
Yet above all, what matters
most is your happiness.
Whatever path you choose,
may it be filled with joy
and fulfillment, for that is
what truly matters in life.*

WEB3 AND BLOCKCHAIN 4 WOMEN
Sanja Kon

Edited and published by The Boss Books/Libri d'Impresa Edizioni

One Hour Marketing Srl
Via Torino 9, 21013 – Gallarate (VA), Italy
www.thebossbooks.com

Copyright @ 2024 Sanja Kon

All rights reserved. This book or parts thereof may not be reproduced
or transmitted in any form by any means
– electronic, mechanical, photocopy, recording, or otherwise –
without prior written permission of the author.

ISBN 9791280622952

Contents

FOREWORD

by Peter Diamandis

Web3 and Blockchain for Women comes at a pivotal moment, as the world stands on the cusp of a technological revolution that promises to redefine the landscape of opportunity and wealth. In an age where exponential technologies are rapidly democratizing the means of production and distribution, *Web3 and Blockchain* stand at the forefront. They offer a decentralized approach, putting the power back into the hands of the individual. It's a shift from scarcity to abundance, from gatekeepers to open doors, and from a privileged few to the empowered many. However, my journey with entrepreneurs worldwide reaffirms that technology's potential is unlocked not by the tools themselves, but by the mindset of those wielding them. The right mindset transforms weaknesses into strengths, challenges into stepping stones, and dreams into realities. That is why I'm so excited about this book. It not only demystifies blockchain technology and gives a practical roadmap to harnessing it but also tackles the crucial aspect of mindset.

An abundance mindset is essential in the tech industry, especially for women, who despite the progress made, remain underrepresented. This mindset sees the future not as a source of insurmountable challenges but as a landscape brimming with opportunities. It understands that the next big idea, the next breakthrough, the next entrepreneurial success story could come from anyone, anywhere, provided they have the tools and the vision to see it through. This book aims to supply both.

Sanja, whom I've come to know as part of Abundance360 community, embodies the principles of abundance, inclusivity, innovation, and entrepreneurship. She witnessed the rapid acceleration of blockchain technologies, understood the implications they hold for economic empowerment, and decided to be a creative force instead of another 'lurker'.

With over 5 billion people now online, the potential for women in terms of collaboration, innovation, and shared success is greater than ever. Sanja's work is an invitation for women to take part in this unfolding narrative of growth and opportunity. Her vision is not just for women to participate in this new era but to lead it. With her guidance, readers will find not just a path to financial independence, but a journey towards a richer, more connected life.

As we look to the future, it's clear that technologies like blockchain will redefine our notions of value, collaboration, and community. They promise a world where every individual has the opportunity to contribute, create, and benefit from the collective advancements of our society. This book is a crucial step in ensuring that women are at the forefront of this transformation.

Web3 and Blockchain 4 women is a beacon for those standing at the threshold of the *Web3* revolution. It is books like Sanja's that will serve as critical touchstones for those seeking to make their mark in the digital domain. It is my sincere hope that this book will inspire you to embrace an abundance mindset, to see the future as a canvas of possibility, and to join a new generation of women investors and entrepreneurs who are using technology to build a better world. The future is abundant, and it awaits your contribution.

INTRODUCTION

Embrace Your Financial Independence!

Many years ago, my grandmother said to me:

"Everything can be taken away from you, except your intelligence and knowledge. Always invest in yourself, as it will allow you to reinvent yourself whenever you need to."

She was a remarkable woman who believed in female empowerment and building personal wealth, even during the challenging times she'd experienced in war-torn Yugoslavia when she lost most of her property and assets overnight. And she'd taught me a valuable lesson.

As a Bosnian refugee, I was challenged by the obstacles of growing up in a foreign country after my family had lost everything. My experience has made me passionate about financial inclusion. I had my own dream, and I came to live that dream by becoming one of the few successful women in financial technology and a major player in the world of *cryptocurrency* and *Web3*.

I've learned to invest in myself.

Intellectual wealth endures, providing strength and resilience even when our circumstances change. This realization was instrumental in shaping my journey. It influenced my decision to learn more about finance and develop an empowering mindset.

In today's rapidly evolving world, where technology and digital advancements shape the future, it's crucial for women to take control of their financial destinies. Yet, due to culture, prejudices, or misguided mindsets, women limit themselves, especially when it comes to their relationship with money.

Financial literacy isn't always taught to women, especially in marginalized regions, for example in Africa only 37% of women possess a bank account[1], resulting in a staggering $42 billion financial

---

1 Hanan Morsy, 'Access to finance: why aren't women leaning in?' March 2020, International Monetary Fund https://www.imf.org/en/Publications/fandd/issues/2020/03/africa-gender-gap-access-to-finance-morsy#:~:text=In%20sub%2DSaharan%20Africa%2C%20only,over%20the%20past%20several%20years [accessed 7 July 2023]

gap between women and men.[2] Although women have assumed more financial management roles and responsibilities over the past two decades, numerous cultures and societies lag behind in promoting gender equality in financial matters. These trends aren't limited to underdeveloped regions; even in Western societies, the idea that men control finance still persists. For example, only 50% of women in the United States maintain a bank account separate from their partner.[3] The global perspective is even worse; nearly 70% of women globally are excluded from financial services.

Society makes women feel inadequate when it comes to handling their own finances. No wonder that two in five women report feeling stressed about their financial situation compared to men.[4] Women face constant uphill battles and getting them to recognize their true value is a constant challenge, despite the fact that women possess qualities that make them exceptional leaders.

I want to help empower women to upgrade their money mindset, take control of their finances and build a solid foundation for their economic well-being. I want to show them how to leverage today's opportunities, gain confidence in making their own financial decisions, and break free from stereotypes that restrict their financial potential.

Imagine a world where women have access to more capital so they can create and scale solutions to global problems. Imagine a world where us women found billion-dollar businesses, and where we can harness our power and build wealth to contribute toward a better world.[5]

This is my dream; this can be our future.

2 Angelique Kidjo, 'Africa: How to Close the $42 Billion Financing Gap Women Face' all Africa, https://allafrica.com/stories/201911190118.html [accessed July 7 2023].
3 'Do you have a bank account separate from your partner?' statista, https://www.statista.com/statistics/1186229/women-with-separate-bank-accounts-usa/ [accessed July 7 2023]
4 Sarah Foster, 'Women are more likely to feel stressed about their finances than men – here's what to do about it' June 1 2022, Bankrate, https://www.bankrate.com/banking/federal-reserve/why-women-feel-more-financial-stress/ [accessed July 7 2023].
5 'Women entrepreneurs in these markets are a trillion-dollar opportunity. Here's why.' (2023, 23 June). World Economic Forum. https://www.weforum.org/agenda/2023/06/women-entrepreneurs-frontier-markets-opportunity/

If you want to improve your relationship with money, this book is for you. If you have financial goals, or simply want to better your understanding of the financial world, you've come to the right place.

It's time to question your beliefs and attitudes toward financial management, so you can overcome the gender inequalities that are constantly thrown your way.

Fortunately, there's a better way of doing things. The economic landscape has changed drastically over the last few years, and advances in technology are poised to reshape the very foundation of our economy. No longer do the same old people hold the reins of economic power. Instead, a decentralized new economy allows for a decentralized approach, encompassing data, finances, and digital identities. The absence of intermediaries and third-party entities fosters cost reduction, heightens transparency, augments accountability, and bolsters security.

We call this new age *Web3*.

This era represents the third generation of the internet. It serves as the decentralized counterpart to its predecessors, incorporating cutting-edge technologies like *blockchain* and *cryptocurrency*. But *Web3*'s essence transcends its technical underpinnings. At its core, *Web3* is a movement toward a fairer internet. It signifies a departure from the clutches of Big Tech and empowers users to reclaim control of their own data. Instead of relying on a single central authority to control and validate transactions, *Web3* uses a network of computers to collectively validate and secure data. This offers enhanced security and resilience, making it more difficult for hackers to control the system.

Blockchain is the underlying technology and brings important benefits, such as transparency through a public ledger. Anyone can see transactions and audit them. Transparency promotes trust and accountability and allows individuals to verify the authenticity and integrity of data without relying on third parties.

Blockchain and *Web3* are now gaining traction because of their unique value propositions. And this makes it the perfect opportunity for a woman seeking to take control of her finances.

But is the *blockchain* really going to spark a financial revolution?

Yes. And here's why.

Many banks and governments have already adopted crypto. Nearly 382 major banks have joined the movement, with more global players expected to follow suit over the next few years.

Digital currencies are becoming more widely accepted in every industry, serving as a real form of payment. From micropayments to large transactions, facilitating the movement of money through *blockchain* is more secure than other methods.

Blockchain is widespread in countries with high inflation rates. Inflation generally drops the value of traditional currency, but digital currency doesn't experience inflationary pressures in the same way as traditional currency. It isn't inflation-proof, but digital currency exhibits significantly lower fluctuations. For example, when the Turkish lira experienced more than 100% inflation, many investors saw *cryptocurrency* as a way to protect their funds.[6]

Understanding the new opportunities that *Web3* and *Blockchain* provide for women requires an open mind. Learning new financial habits, tips, and tricks takes time and effort. Keeping an open mind also helps you think critically and rationally. You may need to step out of your comfort zone to fully utilize *Web3 and Blockchain*.

That's why I decided to write this book. I can walk alongside you as you address the hardships and roadblocks the financial realm places in front of women. I've been able to successfully overcome these challenges, and you can too.

---

6 *'Turkey inflation rate,' Trading Economics, https://tradingeconomics.com/turkey/inflation-cpi [accessed July 7 2023].*

I'm passionate about diversity, inclusion, and continuous improvement, and committed to making a lasting impact on the way people pay. What you're about to read is based on my own experience as a digital executive and entrepreneur. Having built and led international teams in challenging commercial environments has given me a wealth of expertise. I'd like to guide you through this new age. Quite simply, I want to offer you solutions that you can put into action to improve your financial situation.

Like you, I've faced discrimination based on my gender. But the power is yours and you control it. Like me, you can learn how to sell yourself and how to talk to be visible. You can unleash your potential using *Web3 and Blockchain*.

Let's start your journey.

CHAPTER 1

The power of a money mindset: rethinking your financial paradigm

*The past does not
equal your future.*

Tony Robbins

Money does indeed make the world go round, but have you ever stopped to consider who's spinning it? The answer is you. Your mindset about money shapes your financial destiny. It's not just about working hard; it's about working smart. It's about understanding that you are the architect of your own life, and with the right mindset, you can unlock doors you never thought possible.

1. Breaking Free from Societal Constructs

As a child from a communist regime, I wasn't taught about personal wealth creation. At university, I learned about macroeconomics, but this is designed to make white-collar drones become cogs in the wheel of a corporate machine. I realized early in my career that I didn't want to be controlled by corporate practices. I needed to rethink my money mindset.

Women in finance and tech face a unique set of challenges, often stemming from societal constructs that favor men. For example, while men are celebrated for their ambition, women with the same drive are often labeled as 'aggressive' or 'bossy.' These stereotypes hold women back and, difficult though it is, it's crucial to break free from them. You must be unapologetically yourself, even when society tries to put you in a box.

Similarly, one of the most damaging myths is the assumption that men are inherently better at investing and financial management. This false belief can deter women from taking control of their own finances. It's time to challenge these assumptions and heal your relationship with money. Your journey toward financial freedom starts with debunking these myths.

Studies have shown that women are more likely to **outsource financial decision-making and investment management to men**. There's a variety of reasons for this, including lack of confidence, time constraints, or a desire to fulfil a traditional gender role.[7] But outsourcing your financial life means outsourcing your power.

It's even worse for women in emerging countries who often face more barriers to investing compared with those in developed countries. These barriers include limited access to financial services, legal restrictions, and lower financial literacy rates.[8]

When I first picked up Sheryl Sandberg's book, *"Lean In: Women, Work, and the Will to Lead,"* I was surprised by how much it resonated with me, especially when it came to the topic of women and finances. The book made me realize that many of us women underestimate our abilities when it comes to money matters. We often shy away from taking financial risks, perhaps because society has conditioned us to think that finance is a *"man's world".*[9] But it's time we challenge these assumptions. My main insight was that financial independence isn't just about earning money; it's about actively managing it, understanding investments, and making informed decisions. It's not enough to lean in at the workplace; we need to lean into our financial lives as well.

So, if you've been outsourcing your financial decisions to your partner or a financial advisor, maybe it's time to take a more active role. Believe in your capabilities. After all, if someone like me can learn to navigate the complexities of financial planning, there's no reason you can't.

While leaning into our financial lives is crucial, there's a second norm that needs to be questioned: **the traditional blueprint for career success that society has laid out for us**. It's important to challenge

---

7 O'Neill, B., Sorhaindo, B., Xiao, J. J., & Garman, E. T. (2005). 'Women's decision-making roles regarding household financial matters and National Endowment for Financial Education', "Gender Differences in Investment Decision-Making," (2016).
8 World Bank, 'Gender, Poverty, and Access to Financial Services in West Africa and World Economic Forum' The Global Gender Gap Report 2017
9 Sandberg, Sheryl author. (2013). 'Lean in: women, work, and the will to lead'. New York: Random House Audio

this norm, because as it is ingrained in us, and many women will not dare to venture out of this very narrow path. Growing up, we're often told that the key to a successful career is a linear path: excel in school, get into a prestigious university, and then land a high-paying job in a big corporation. This narrative is deeply ingrained in us, almost like a societal blueprint for success. But let's pause and challenge this norm for a moment.

I think Robert Kiyosaki's book *"Rich Dad Poor Dad"*, summarizes the situation in the best way possible. Kiyosaki tells the story of his two dads: one rich, one poor. One had poor academic credentials, the other had an impressive list of degrees. Here is the catch: the poor one was his father who was highly educated with a regular income job, the rich one was the father of his friend who didn't have an amazing list of diplomas but was a self-taught business man. What differentiated both, his father was well educated on paper but did not have the skills or means to get out of the *"rat race"*, an endless cycle of earning and spending. On the other hand, the father with poor formal education was financially literate and knew how to make money working for him instead of chasing it.[10] This story shattered for me the myth that formal education is the only route to financial success. It made me realize that following the traditional path could very well lead us to become *"poor dads"*, trapped in the cycle of earning and spending without ever achieving true financial freedom.

Even though I will delve into why this traditional idea of success can be misleading in later chapters, I'd like to share some initial thoughts here. First off, many people we consider **successful today are university dropouts** or never even set foot in a university. Think of Steve Jobs or Bill Gates, their journeys debunk the myth that a prestigious university is the only gateway to success. The crux of the matter is skills.

10 Kiyosaki, R. T. (2017). 'Rich dad, poor dad' (2nd ed.). Plata Publishing.

In the time we invest in university studies or clocking in extra hours at a corporate job, we could be learning invaluable skills that are actually relevant in the 21st century. Skills that could exponentially grow our income beyond a regular pay check.

In the context of challenging the traditional career blueprint we also have to address the **notion that success is solely measured by a hefty pay check**. In these high-pressure jobs, work-life balance and mental health often take a backseat. We end up spending a disproportionate amount of time working, usually in stressful environments. What's the point of earning well if you can't enjoy the life those earnings are supposed to provide?

The most disheartening part? Many times, the work doesn't even feel meaningful. During my stint in the corporate world, I often felt like just another cog in the machine, easily replaceable and devoid of purpose, even as I climbed the corporate ladder.

But there are alternatives. Freelancing and entrepreneurship, for instance, offer different but equally valid paths to success. These options are often less talked about but can be more rewarding in many ways.

These were just some initial thoughts, as we move forward let's redefine what success means to us. Let's challenge societal norms and carve out our own paths. Because, at the end of the day, it's not about fitting into a pre-defined role; it's about creating a life that aligns with your values and aspirations. Let's explore together where to start.

1.1 Start with why

In order to carve out your own path, rather than walking one laid out for you by others , it is essential to deeply understand yourself. What drives you? What's your core motivation?

As Simon Sinek would put it, you have to: *"Start with why"*.[11] The journey of self-discovery can be deeply personal and challenging, often tied to emotional or sensitive topics from one's personal or family history. But it is essential as it will give you the necessary energy to keep going when you face challenges. (And believe me you will)

One effective method to uncover your *"why"* is the **"5 Whys"** technique. It's a simple problem-solving method that helps you get to the root cause of an issue by asking *"Why?"* five times. Each answer forms the basis of the next question.

We start this exploration with the following declaration: *"I want to be financially independent and in control!"* Here is an example:

1. **Why** do I want to be financially independent and in control?
   Because I want the freedom to make my own choices without relying on anyone else.

2. **Why** do I want the freedom to make my own choices?
   Because I've always felt constrained by my family's expectations and societal norms.

3. **Why** have I felt constrained by these expectations and norms?
   Because my parents had a traditional view of what a woman's role should be, and I felt like I had to fit into that mold.

4. **Why** did their traditional view affect me so deeply?
   Because I love and respect my parents, but I also felt that their expectations were limiting my potential and happiness.

5. **Why** is it so important for me to unlock my potential and find happiness?
   Because I believe that I have unique talents and perspectives to offer the world, and fulfilling that potential is my path to true happiness and self-worth.

11 Sinek, Simon. 2011. 'Start with Why'. Harlow, England: Penguin Books.

Many times, we start this exercise with motivations that are external or related to status, and that's completely okay. It's often easier to acknowledge these surface-level drivers. However, it's crucial to understand that this is just the starting point. As you dig deeper with each *"Why"*, you'll likely transition from extrinsic motivations to more intrinsic ones that get to the core of your being.

While the method is traditionally called the *"5 Whys"*, don't feel restricted by the number. If you find that asking a sixth or even seventh *"Why"* provides deeper insights, go for it. You can also repeat this exercise multiple times to confirm that you consistently arrive at the same root motivation.

If you find it challenging to do this exercise alone, consider asking a trusted friend or family member to ask the *"Why"* questions for you. Just make sure to explain the context beforehand. It's important that the person maintains a neutral expression, free of judgment, to allow for honest introspection.

Once you've identified your *"Why,"* make it visible in your daily life. Write it in large letters and place it in your office, or set it as your phone's wallpaper. The idea is to keep it somewhere you'll see regularly.

Your *"Why"* statement might look something like this:

"I want to be in charge of my own financial destiny because..." followed by your deeper, intrinsic motivation.

After identifying my "Why", I realized that my journey towards financial independence was deeply influenced by my upbringing and the societal norms I was exposed to. My *"Why"* is rooted in a desire for personal freedom and self-expression, a yearning born from a childhood where financial education was absent and traditional roles were enforced.

It took me some time to understand that owning a business wasn't a privilege reserved for men or those born into affluence. My path from a naïve child refugee, indoctrinated with a limiting ideology, to a self-sufficient, independent businesswoman was arduous but enlightening. My passion for technologies and services that foster financial freedom stems from the lack of financial education I received as a child. Growing up in communist Bosnia during the Tito era, my parents were products of an oppressive regime that traded personal freedom for a false sense of security. In this environment, the government met basic needs like food, shelter, and employment, but at the expense of individual liberties such as freedom of speech, creativity, and personal enterprise.

This lack of financial autonomy extended into my family life as well. My father kept financial matters a secret from my mother, leaving her powerless and confined in a challenging marriage. I knew I wanted a different future, and that's why I embarked on a journey toward greater financial freedom.

So, there you have it – that's my *"Why"*. It's a deeply personal motivation that fuels my every action and decision. I share this with you to show you that your *"Why"* can be a powerful catalyst for change. Now that we've established our *"Why"*, it's crucial to delve deeper into our money mindset. Understanding the *"Why"* gives us the foundation, but to build a stable structure of financial independence, we need to explore our attitudes, beliefs, and behaviors surrounding money. And that's exactly what we'll do next.

2. What does money mean to you? Your Money Mindset

One of the most pivotal steps on your journey to financial independence is understanding your unique relationship with money, or what we'll refer to as your *"money mindset"*. Early on in my financial journey, I realized that if I wanted to make more money, I needed to understand what money truly meant to me. This is a lesson that holds true for everyone. Your money mindset serves as your mental blueprint, shaping your financial behaviors, attitudes, and ultimately, your financial destiny.

This mindset isn't something you consciously choose; it's a complex tapestry woven from various threads – your upbringing, societal norms, personal experiences, and even subconscious beliefs you might not be fully aware of. For instance, if you grew up in a household where money was always tight, you might subconsciously associate money with stress or scarcity. Conversely, if you were raised in an environment where financial discussions were open and educational, you might view money as a tool for creating opportunities and freedom.

Your money mindset often correlates directly with your wealth. And by wealth, we don't necessarily mean your monthly income. There are individuals who earn substantial amounts but have a negative money mindset that compels them to spend it all. They might fear money because they don't know how to manage large amounts, or they might associate it with moral corruption, thinking that being rich equates to being a bad person.

Here's an eye-opening fact: a significant number of lottery winners end up losing all their winnings within a few years. Why does this happen? It's because they didn't have the mindset to manage that wealth. Becoming wealthy and financially independent isn't just about accumulating money; it's about cultivating a mindset that enables you to make sound financial decisions.

Uncovering these deeply ingrained thoughts about money will require some effort, as they are often hidden in the recesses of your subconscious mind. But it's an effort worth making. If you fear money or think that having a lot of it is inherently bad, you'll find it difficult to hold onto it, let alone grow it. Your mindset dictates how you interact with money on a daily basis. It influences your earning potential, your spending habits, and your ability to save and invest.

You might think you're in control and making conscious decisions about your finances, but studies have shown that much of our decision-making is actually done on autopilot. This means that many times, we're not guided by rational thought but by our subconscious beliefs. Understanding your money mindset is crucial because it programs this *"autopilot"* mode. If your mindset is tuned to a frequency of financial limitation, you'll find that no matter what opportunities come your way, you'll unconsciously sabotage yourself to stay within those limits. Therefore, it's essential to program your autopilot in a way that aligns with your financial goals and aspirations.

Before we move on to the exercise designed to help you uncover and transform your money mindset, let's acknowledge that understanding your relationship with money is a deeply personal and often emotionally charged endeavor. This is why the exercise we're about to undertake is so crucial. It's not just about identifying your beliefs; it's about transforming them into a mindset that serves your financial aspirations.

2.1 Uncovering and Transforming Your Money Mindset

Now that we've laid the groundwork, in the next section we'll delve into practical exercises designed to help you unearth your current thoughts and feelings about money. This exercise will not only reveal your existing mindset but also guide you in reshaping it into a more empowering one.

2.1.1 Identifying your money mindset

Instructions

1. **Set the Stage:** find a quiet space where you won't be disturbed. Have a pen and paper or a digital note-taking app ready.

2. **Time Constraint:** this exercise is most effective when done quickly to capture your immediate, gut-level responses. Set a timer for 10 minutes.

3. **Answer the Questions:** below are a series of questions and sentences designed to probe your thoughts and feelings about money. Write down the first thing that comes to mind for each question. Don't overthink it; your initial response is often the most telling.
   - What does money symbolize for you?
   - At its essence, money is...?
   - I... money because... (fill out this sentence)
   - Money can...?
   - Money can't...?
   - Accumulating money will lead to...?
   - Without money I am...
   - What does affluence mean to you?
   - Being rich means...
   - What would being extremely rich signify for you?
   - Being wealthy means...?
   - More money would allow me to...?
   - What are your primary motivations for wanting money?
   - What are you prepared to do to earn money?
   - What steps are you willing to take to master your finances?
   - Ultimately, what role does money play in your life?

4. **Review Your Answers:** once the timer goes off, stop writing. Take a moment to review your answers. Do you notice any patterns or recurring themes? Take a few minutes to reflect on this exercise. Did anything surprise you? Were there any 'aha' moments? Write down those insights as you move on later to Part 2: Shifting Your Money Mindset.

Remember, the goal here is not to judge yourself but to gain a clearer understanding of your current mindset. This is the first step in transforming your relationship with money. Now that you've identified your existing beliefs, you're ready to make the next step, where we'll work on shifting those beliefs towards abundance.

2.1.2 From Scarcity to Abundance

Now that we've identified your money mindset, it's time to delve deeper into understanding and transforming it. At the core of this transformation lies the distinction between two primary types of mindsets: the **Scarcity Mindset** and the **Abundance Mindset**. These represent two extremes on a spectrum, and while many of us may find ourselves somewhere in between, our goal is to shift more towards an abundance mindset.

Scarcity Mindset is characterized by the belief that there's a limited number of resources available. This perspective sees life as a finite pie, meaning if one person gets a bigger slice, there's less for everyone else. Such a mindset often stems from experiences in competitive environments, like the corporate world, where promotions and raises are rare, resources are limited, and short-term thinking prevails. This mentality can hinder us from achieving our goals and realizing our full potential.

On the other hand, the **Abundance Mindset** is rooted in the belief that there's plenty out there for everyone. It focuses on gratitude for what one has and the possibilities that lie ahead. Instead of seeing limitations, it sees opportunities. This mindset believes in the vastness of resources and opportunities available to all. It's about recognizing the wealth of possibilities and being grateful for whatever the universe provides. Tony Robbins emphasizes that an abundance mindset allows you to focus on what you already have, making peace with the present moment. By not living in a state of fear, you can experience the many benefits of gratitude, make better decisions, and plan for the future.

Even if we achieve financial success, it's crucial to recognize and appreciate the abundance already present in our lives. If we're always chasing bigger numbers without acknowledging the wealth around us, we'll find ourselves in a never-ending cycle of wanting more. Recognizing the abundance in our current circumstances ensures that when we do achieve financial milestones, we can genuinely appreciate and enjoy them.

Exercise - Shifting Your Money Mindset

1. **Identify Your Current Mindset:** reflect on the money mindset you've uncovered earlier. Is it leaning more towards scarcity or abundance?

2. **Acceptance:** if you find that your mindset is one of scarcity, that's okay. Recognizing it is the first step towards transformation. Remember, everyone starts somewhere.

3. **Transform Your Affirmations:** take the affirmations or beliefs you've identified and reframe them into positive ones that reflect abundance. For example, if you wrote in part one of the exercise that accumulating wealth makes you feel

guilty, your affirmation might be, *"It's okay to desire financial abundance"*. Or, for instance, if you previously thought, *"I'll never have enough money"*, transform it into, *"Money flows easily and abundantly to me"*.

By actively working on shifting your mindset from scarcity to abundance, you're setting the foundation for not only financial success but also a fulfilling and contented life.

2.2 Maintaining a Healthy Abundance Money Mindset

Recognizing and shifting towards an abundance mindset is just the beginning. Like any transformation, it requires consistent effort and practice to maintain and nurture. Here's how you can ensure that your abundance mindset remains robust and continues to serve you well:

1. **Practice Gratitude Daily:** one of the most effective ways to cultivate an abundance mindset is by acknowledging and appreciating what you already have. Start or end your day by listing three things you're grateful for. This simple act can shift your focus from what you lack to what you possess.

2. **Create an Abundance Account:** set up a special account dedicated solely to nurturing your abundance mindset. Commit to saving a fraction of your income in this account every month. The purpose of this account is to spend on experiences or items that make you feel wealthy and fulfilled. Whether it's indulging in a lavish dinner at an exquisite restaurant, enjoying a weekend getaway at a luxurious hotel, investing in quality clothing, or even contributing to a charity that resonates with you, the aim is to materialize your gratitude. The only rule? Make sure to spend this money either to reward yourself or to give back to the world. Don't let it overaccumulate.

You can save it for a bigger donation or purchase, but set yourself a clear goal with a fix number. As soon as you reach that number spend it all. This practice not only reinforces your sense of abundance but also allows you to tangibly experience the joys that come with it.

3. **Surround Yourself with Positive Influences:** your environment plays a significant role in shaping your mindset. Engage with people who uplift you and share your values of abundance. Avoid naysayers or those who perpetually see the glass as half empty.

4. **Reframe Challenges as Opportunities:** instead of viewing obstacles as setbacks, see them as chances to learn and grow. This perspective shift can help you approach problems with a more open and optimistic mindset.

5. **Affirm Your Abundance:** use positive affirmations from the previous exercise to reinforce your abundance mindset.

As we journey through the landscape of our financial beliefs, understanding our abundance mindset is just one piece of the puzzle. Another equally pivotal aspect? Our risk tolerance. Think of it this way: if our mindset is the compass guiding our financial journey, our risk tolerance is the terrain we're comfortable traversing.

3. Navigating the Terrain of Risk

As we continue our journey towards financial prosperity, it's essential to understand and embrace the inherent risks that come with financial decisions. Whether you're considering launching a start-up, diving into the world of investments, or pivoting your financial strategies, it all boils down to one fundamental question: how comfortable are you with risk? Your risk tolerance, an integral facet of your money mindset, plays a pivotal role in shaping your financial well-being.

Imagine this example: you've recently invested in *cryptocurrency* based on a friend's recommendation, without fully grasping its fundamentals. As the market ebbs and flows, you find yourself anxiously watching the screen, your heartbeat mirroring the erratic price fluctuations. This situation might resonate with some and let it serve as a cautionary tale. Investing based on someone else's advice – be it a friend, a YouTuber, or anyone not qualified – is in general not a good idea. It can lead you down a perilous path. In this context specifically, the emotional turmoil you experience is a glaring indicator that the investment doesn't align with your risk tolerance. In essence, your fear of losing money overshadows your confidence in long-term gains. The key takeaway? Always align your financial decisions with your own comfort level regarding risk, ensuring your peace of mind remains intact throughout your financial journey.

3.1 Understanding your risk tolerance

Risk tolerance is your personal comfort level with the potential outcomes of an investment. It's a blend of your financial ability to withstand losses and your emotional capacity to endure the roller coaster of market ups and downs. Everyone's risk tolerance is unique, shaped by factors like age, financial situation, investment goals, and life experiences.

According to Forbes[12], risk tolerance can be categorized into three main types:

- Conservative: investors who prioritize safety over returns. They prefer stable investments and are averse to significant losses.

- Moderate: investors who seek a balance between safety and returns. They're willing to accept some losses in pursuit of higher returns.

- Aggressive: investors who prioritize high returns and are comfortable with substantial risks. They're more tolerant of short-term losses in hopes of long-term gains.

Risk tolerance isn't just a label; it's a spectrum. To pinpoint where you fall on this spectrum, there are online risk assessment tests available, like the one provided by the University of Missouri: Investment Risk Tolerance Assessment[13]. Such tools can offer an initial insight into your risk profile.

Alternatively, introspective questions can also guide your understanding:

- Do financial decisions make you anxious?

- How long is your investment time horizon?

- Are you willing to take on more risk for the potential of higher return?

- How would you respond if the value of your investments declined significantly?

- Do you have the discipline to stick to your investment strategy in a difficult market cycle?

- Would you feel pressured to sell out of your positions or to sell your company if the economy gets difficult?

12 Baldridge, R. (2023, May 8). 'What Is Your Risk Tolerance?' Forbes. Retrieved from https://www.forbes.com/advisor/investing/what-is-your-risk-tolerance/
13 https://cafnr.missouri.edu/divisions/division-of-applied-social-sciences/research/investment-risk-tolerance-assessment/

It's crucial to remember that risk tolerance isn't static. As you transition through different life stages, your financial goals and comfort with risk may evolve. For instance, younger individuals might be more inclined to take risks, given the longer investment horizon ahead of them. In contrast, those nearing retirement might prioritize preserving their capital.

However, it's essential to recognize that your current level of risk has played a significant role in shaping your present financial situation. If you maintain the exact same risk level, you might find yourself stagnating, unable to move forward from where you started. Embracing an abundance mindset means not only recognizing opportunities but also having the courage to seize them. Thus, the question is: how can we increase our risk level?

3.2 Increasing Your Risk Level

One practical approach to increasing your risk tolerance is to establish a **financial safety net**. By setting aside six months' worth of living expenses in a savings account, you create a buffer against unforeseen financial challenges. This reserve not only provides peace of mind but also grants you the freedom to venture outside your comfort zone without the constant worry of immediate financial repercussions. With this safety net in place, you're better equipped to take calculated risks, knowing you have a fallback should things not go as planned.

Once your safety net is set up, you can start with embracing **incremental risk-taking**. Start by taking small, calculated risks that you can comfortably manage. As you gain experience and confidence, you can progressively scale up to more significant challenges and investments. This incremental approach not only helps you become more comfortable with risk but also provides valuable learning experiences that prepare you for bigger opportunities. With each successful venture, you'll find that your capacity to handle risk expands, along with your appetite for greater rewards.

Another effective strategy to elevate your risk tolerance is **diversification**. The age-old affirmation, *"Don't put all your eggs in one basket"*, holds true when it comes to financial planning. By spreading your investments across various asset classes – be it stocks, bonds, real estate, or even cryptocurrencies – you mitigate the risk associated with market volatility. Diversification doesn't just cushion potential losses; it also offers multiple avenues for growth. When one sector of your portfolio underperforms, another might be thriving, balancing out the overall impact and allowing you to maintain a steadier financial course.

Often, our risk tolerance is a manifestation of our fears. And what is fear, if not the unknown? The unfamiliar terrains of investments, business decisions, or even personal challenges can be daunting. The antidote to this fear is knowledge. By continuously acquiring new skills and expanding our understanding, we demystify the unknown, transforming it into a known quantity. This process not only alleviates fear but also equips us with the tools and confidence to navigate challenges more effectively. We'll delve deeper into this concept in Chapter 2.

As we've explored ways to increase your risk tolerance through financial safety nets, diversification, and knowledge, it's crucial to remember that even the best-laid plans can encounter unexpected challenges. While we strive to mitigate risks, life's unpredictability means that financial crises can still occur. How we respond to these crises often reveals the true mettle of our financial preparedness and mindset. Let's delve into how to navigate such turbulent waters when they arise.

3.3 Being hit by a sudden personal financial crisis

Even with the right money mindset and diligent efforts to educate yourself about personal finance, a sudden financial crisis can still strike unexpectedly. The true test isn't the amount of money you've lost, but rather how you react to the situation. As a child, my family lost everything in a war, leaving me grappling with feelings of powerlessness and confusion. This formative experience has deeply influenced my approach to financial crises, instilling in me a determination to never feel that helpless again.

Staying calm and objective

The first critical step in weathering a financial storm is to remain calm and objective. In moments of panic, people often make impulsive decisions, such as liquidating assets without fully understanding the broader financial context. It's essential to pause, take a deep breath, and assess the situation methodically. Identify the root cause of the crisis, evaluate its immediate and long-term impact on your finances, and prioritize the issues that require urgent attention.

Understanding market cycles

Overconfidence can be a silent killer, especially if you've entered the market during a bullish phase. Markets are inherently cyclical; they have their ups and downs. Recognizing this can help you avoid the pitfalls of overconfidence and the subsequent losses in a bear market.

Learning and growing

The silver lining of any personal financial crisis is the opportunity it provides for self-reflection and growth. Such crises force you to re-evaluate your financial strategies and learn from your mistakes. They can serve as a wake-up call, prompting you to reassess your risk tolerance, diversify your investment portfolio, and perhaps most importantly, examine your money mindset.

What to remember

- **Mindset matters:** our relationship with money, often referred to as your "money mindset," is shaped by various factors including your upbringing, societal norms, personal experiences, and subconscious beliefs. This mindset plays a pivotal role in determining your financial destiny.

- **Breaking societal constructs:** societal constructs can limit our potential. It's crucial to challenge these assumptions and stereotypes, especially for women.

- **Start with why:** understand your core motivation. The *"5 Whys"* technique can help you uncover your intrinsic motivations that drive your financial decisions.

- **Change your mind:** to achieve financial success, it's crucial to understand and positively transform your money mindset. To pave the way towards an abundance mindset, begin by identifying your current beliefs about money. Once recognized, actively work to shift any negative perceptions into positive self-affirmations.

This transformation is key to fostering
a healthy and prosperous relationship
with finances.

- **Cultivating an Abundance Money Mindset:**
  like a garden your abundance mindset
  needs maintenance. Regularly use positive
  affirmations to reinforce and maintain
  this mindset. Also surround yourself
  with positive influences and consistently
  practice gratitude by acknowledging what
  you have.

- **Navigating risk:** understand your risk
  tolerance. It's a blend of your financial
  ability to withstand losses and your
  emotional capacity to endure market
  fluctuations.

CHAPTER 2

Seeking knowledge: cultivating your education in the bitcoin economy

Schools teach you how to work for money, but don't teach how to make money work for you.

Robert Kiyosaki

Our path to financial prosperity is closely tied to a commitment to **continuous learning.** Diving into the realms of investment or entrepreneurship without adequate knowledge is not just risky—it's a gamble. While you might find guidance from third-party advisors, this approach often means ceding control of your financial future to someone else, which is far from the ideal route to lasting financial freedom.

Achieving lasting financial independence is a **long-term commitment that necessitates a learning attitude**. This mindset is fueled by curiosity, a thirst for knowledge, and the patience to build a solid foundation of wisdom for your financial success. In this framework, setbacks transform into learning opportunities, and successes are analyzed to understand how they can be consistently replicated.

It's crucial to **exercise patience** and avoid promises of shortcuts to wealth.

These shortcuts can be deeply ingrained in your culture. For instance, I was born in a traditional culture where women were often encouraged to marry into financial security. While this may appear to be an easy route, it's fraught with risks and perpetuates a culture that undermines financial inclusivity. In such a setup, you're always one misstep away from financial instability, dependent on someone else's financial decisions. The same caution should be exercised when confronted with the myriad *"get rich quick"* schemes and courses that populate the online space.

These shortcuts are tempting but rarely lead to sustainable wealth.

In this chapter, we'll delve into the educational principles and skills essential for achieving your financial goals. I'll guide you on how to carve out your own educational path and discern the type of education that will genuinely benefit you.

But before we get into that, let's first examine the limitations of traditional educational systems that often fall short in preparing us for real-world financial challenges.

1. The limitations of traditional path

The **traditional educational** path often starts with rigorous academic preparation, aimed ideally at gaining admission to a prestigious university. Once there, the focus shifts to excelling in courses that, in theory, should prepare you for a well-paying corporate job. The journey doesn't end with graduation; it continues into the workplace, where you're expected to acquire new skills, often through company-mandated training programs. Eventually, you might ascend to a managerial role, where the skills that initially made you valuable become secondary to administrative tasks. However, this progression is usually accompanied by a higher pay check, which seems to justify the journey but often leaves much to be desired in terms of personal and financial growth.

Starting with the **university experience**, let's pause and critically examine this traditional educational path in the context of tech, finance, and entrepreneurship. My relationship with formal education is a tale of two halves. On one hand, I was fortunate to receive a scholarship to a prestigious Italian university, which provided invaluable social and networking opportunities. On the flip side, if I'm being honest, I can't say that I've used even 1% of what I learned academically in my current endeavors.

So, what exactly are people paying for when they enroll in a university? Top universities can charge tuition fees ranging from $10,000 to $100,000 per year. If you're not planning an academic career as a researcher, you're not really paying for education. Let's be clear: graduating from a prestigious university doesn't make you a genius. It merely indicates that you've navigated a particular system successfully. Traditional educational institutions often miss the mark in one critical area: practical application. They may offer courses in finance but get bogged down in the complexities of macro and microeconomics, often neglecting the practical aspects of money management and investing. The exorbitant tuition fees really raise questions about the true value of this education. Are students really paying for knowledge, or are they buying a brand name to flaunt on their LinkedIn profiles in hopes of gaining a competitive edge in the job market? As mentioned in chapter one, your success is not predetermined by your degrees. Elon Musk is self-taught, and many other tech leaders are college dropouts.

The limitations extend beyond academia into the **corporate world**. When you enter the workforce, especially in a large corporation, your learning path is often predetermined. Initial onboarding programs and subsequent training are usually one-size-fits-all, with little regard for individual aptitude or interest. Even when you have some choice in your learning, it's often guided by the company's needs rather than your own career aspirations. Your manager or HR department might encourage you to acquire skills that serve your team's immediate goals, but these may not necessarily align with your long-term objectives. They justify these training choices by promising you higher chances of getting promoted. But I've heard countless stories from friends and colleagues who were passed over for promotions in favor of external hires, despite having invested time and effort in company-sponsored training programs. And even if you make it into a managerial position, as mentioned at the beginning of this section, most of your previously acquired **skills become obsolete** because now you spend time managing people, going from meeting to meeting, and answering countless emails. The danger lies actually here: once you are in a middle management position and have been trained for it, you become easily replaceable. As we saw during the post-COVID tech layoffs, those who were most affected were middle managers, not the *"productive"* workforce at the bottom of the corporate hierarchy. This raises questions about the efficacy of such educational paths. Are they designed to nurture individual growth, or are they merely mechanisms to produce a predictable, albeit limited, set of skills that serve the company's immediate needs and can be laid off when no longer needed?

Here is the takeaway: the issue with traditional education, both academic and corporate, is that it often lacks **personalization and practical application**. It's a system that I believe is fundamentally flawed, not because it fails to produce intelligent individuals, but because it often produces individuals who are intelligent in ways that serve the system itself, rather than the learners. This isn't to say that everyone coming out of these institutions is devoid of real-world skills; rather that the system is designed more for its own perpetuation than for the benefit of the individual.

In the end, **your education should serve you**, not just the institutions you pass through. It's time to take ownership of your learning journey, to seek out the skills and knowledge that will genuinely serve your life goals and financial aspirations.

2. Exploring Alternatives

Let's give credit where credit is due: for many, including myself, university has been a pivotal stepping stone towards social ascension. It has transformed lives, lifting countless individuals and entire families out of poverty. I wholeheartedly support and commend those who see university as their chosen path. However, it is important that pursuing higher education, as any other learning path, should be a conscious choice, not simply a default decision or a rite of passage.

You have to ask yourself: is this genuinely the best choice for me? If the answer is *"no"* there are many alternative learning avenues. From online courses and mentorship programs to diligent self-study, myriad ways exist to acquire the practical knowledge essential for making informed financial and entrepreneurial decisions. Even if you embrace formal education, always remain receptive to knowledge from diverse sources. This approach ensures that you not only have a solid academic foundation but also the practical skills that align with your financial goals and risk tolerance.

2.1 Books: The Power of 3

One of the most accessible and effective ways to gain knowledge is through reading. You might have heard of the *"3-book rule"*. a concept popularized by Tim Ferriss in his book *"The 4-Hour Work Week"*.[14] While someone with a PhD or an expert in a field might scoff at the idea, consider this: if you read a high-quality book on permaculture, you'll likely know more about the subject than 99% of the people within a 5 km radius of you. Reading 3 books on a topic might not make you a top-tier expert, but it will elevate you to an *"expert amateur"* level. This means you will understand the jargon and be able to engage in meaningful discussions with professionals in the field.

When it comes to **selecting the right books**, it's essential to approach it strategically. Start with an *"explainer book",* one that provides a comprehensive overview of your chosen topic. This book should lay the foundation and give you a fair understanding of the subject matter. Next, move on to a *"practical book"*, one that offers actionable applications of your newfound knowledge. This book should be more hands-on, guiding you through methods or techniques. Finally, dive into a *"thought-provoking book"* one that challenges the status quo

14 Ferriss, Timothy. 'The 4-Hour Workweek' Random House, 2011.

and presents a paradigm shift in your topic. This book should make you question common beliefs and practices, offering a fresh perspective that reopens your mind after you've formed your initial ideas.

While the rule of 3 is a good starting point, don't feel confined by it. If you find that reading more books serves your purpose, by all means, go for it. Turn the rule of 3 into the rule of 5 or even 10. The key is to keep expanding your knowledge base in a way that serves you best.

Now, you might be thinking, *"Sanja, where am I supposed to **find the time to read 3 books?**"* It's a valid concern. Our lives are busy, and carving out reading time can be challenging. But with a bit of creativity, it's doable. We often spend hours on our smartphones, scrolling through articles or being fed content by social media algorithms. Why not reclaim some of that time for reading, even if it's just a page a day? You'll be surprised at the progress you make. Alternatively, audiobooks offer a more passive way to consume content. Switch from radio to an audiobook during your commute, and you'll be amazed at how much you can learn. Remember, starting with three books is just the beginning. As your thirst for knowledge grows, so will your reading list. And by finishing this book, you're already one step closer – only 2 more to go!

2.2 Coaching and seminars: surrounding yourself with the right people

Many times, individuals find themselves at a crossroads, unsure of their passions and what truly drives them. In such instances, working with a coach can be incredibly beneficial. Coaching and seminars play a pivotal role in not only helping you discover your true calling but also in surrounding yourself with the right people. I continue to invest in coaching to maintain a positive mindset and attend seminars for fresh insights and networking. These experiences provide more than just knowledge; they offer a sense of community, especially during challenging times. Engaging in these sessions allows you to learn from others' journeys, helping you navigate your path more effectively and avoid potential pitfalls.

2.2.1 Coaching vs. Therapy: Understanding the nuances to make an informed choice

Many people ask me what the difference is between coaching and therapy. While these two realms are distinct, they sometimes intersect, making it crucial to understand their unique characteristics and objectives. Both can be invaluable tools for your personal development, but they serve different needs and operate on different timelines. Here's a more in-depth look at the two:

Coaching: coaching primarily focuses on the present and the future, aiming to help individuals set and achieve specific goals in areas such as professional development, personal growth, and leadership skills. Coaches often use questioning techniques to guide you toward your own solutions, providing a structured, goal-oriented approach. These relationships are usually short-term and specific to particular objectives. Coaches come from a variety of professional backgrounds and may specialize in different domains. It's important to note that the coaching industry is not universally regulated, although accrediting bodies like the International Coaching Federation (ICF) do set ethical and professional standards.

Therapy: in contrast, therapy delves into the past to address emotional wounds, traumas, and mental health issues with the aim of providing emotional healing and improving overall well-being. Therapists use a range of psychological techniques to help you understand your feelings, behaviors, and thought patterns. Unlike coaching, therapy often involves a longer-term commitment, sometimes extending over years, depending on the complexity of the issues and the progress made. Therapists are licensed mental health professionals, and the industry is regulated, ensuring a certain level of competency and ethical conduct.

While coaching and therapy serve different primary functions, they can sometimes overlap. For example, a life coach might help you explore career options while indirectly improving your emotional well-being. Similarly, a therapist might provide you with practical strategies for stress management that have immediate real-world applications. In summary, the choice between coaching and therapy should be based on your specific needs, goals, and the issues you wish to address. Both can offer valuable insights and tools for personal growth, but they do so from different angles and with different methodologies.

2.2.2 Are you coachable? The first step to effective coaching

Before diving into the world of coaching, it's crucial to ask yourself: ***"Am I coachable?"*** Being coachable means having the willingness and ability to receive feedback and guidance to enhance your personal or professional development. No one can *"force"* you into coaching; it must be a personal choice that excites you. Being coachable involves an open mindset, a willingness to be vulnerable, and letting go of the ego. Here are some questions to ponder:

- Am I open-minded and receptive to new ideas and perspectives?
- Am I willing to challenge my existing beliefs and consider different approaches?
- Do I have a genuine desire to acquire new knowledge and insights?
- Am I ready to acknowledge that there's always room for growth?

- Am I willing to actively listen to and apply the feedback I receive?

If coaching doesn't resonate immediately with you, that's okay. Do your research, talk to people who have undergone coaching, and make an informed decision.

2.2.3 How to choose the right coach

Once you've determined that you're open to coaching, the next step is to find the right coach. Here are some factors to consider:

- **Reputation:** *look for testimonials or reviews from previous clients.*

- **Expertise:** *ensure they have a proven track record in the area you're interested in.*

- **Alignment:** *their values and teaching style should resonate with you.*

- **Accreditation:** *given that the industry is not well-regulated, look for professional accreditations like ICF (International Coaching Federation).*

I often seek recommendations from my network. A coach who has successfully worked with someone I know, is likely to be effective for me as well. Be wary of scammers promising unrealistic outcomes; if it sounds too good to be true, it probably is.

If coaching doesn't resonate immediately with you, or if financial constraints make it less accessible, that's okay. Alternatively, you can seek for a mentor, someone you admire and ideally an individual who is just a handful of steps ahead on the path you aspire to walk. Usually when you reach out for guidance, you will be surprised that many are happy to give back and dedicate some time to mentor others.

2.3 Seminars: a complementary approach

Seminars offer another avenue for growth, often providing fresh insights and valuable networking opportunities. When choosing a seminar, apply the same criteria you would for selecting a coach: reputation, expertise, and alignment with your goals.

2.4 Online Education: the World at Your Fingertips

We're living in a transformative era where the digital landscape has democratized education, making it more accessible than ever. The beauty of online education lies in its unparalleled **flexibility**. Unlike traditional educational systems, which operate on rigid schedules, online courses empower you to learn at your own pace. This is a game-changer, especially for those juggling other life commitments like work or family. It allows you to customize your educational journey, making learning an accessible endeavor for all.

Another advantage of online education is the **sense of community** it fosters. Many courses feature forums or discussion boards, providing a platform for you to engage with like-minded individuals. These communities are not just add-ons; they're integral to the learning experience. They offer a space for networking, collaborative projects, and intellectual exchange, enriching your understanding of the subject matter. This sense of camaraderie can be invaluable, particularly when you're exploring a new or complex topic.

However, the **unregulated nature** of online education is a double-edged sword. While it opens doors for many, it also paves the way for potential scams or low-quality courses. So, how do you navigate this labyrinth of options?

Start by conducting a **self-assessment**. Identify your passions and the skills you're keen to acquire. This self-directed approach will help you narrow down your choices. Once you've honed in on your interests, it's time to do some **investigation**. If you want to select a paid offer, research multiple platforms, scrutinize testimonials, and check for affiliations with reputable institutions.

Many courses offer **free trials** or sample lessons, so seize these opportunities to evaluate their quality. If you're still on the fence, seek recommendations from trusted sources or professionals in the field. Via LinkedIn for example, you can connect with people who've walked the path you're considering.

Don't underestimate the power of **free resources either**. YouTube, often relegated to entertainment, is a goldmine of educational content. Whether it's tutorials, podcasts, or expert talks, the platform offers a wealth of knowledge, often at no cost.

If you are craving a more structured approach, non-profit organizations like Khan Academy offer meticulously organized curricula on a wide array of subjects. Their interactive modules and high-quality videos provide an educational experience that can rival even traditional institutions.

The beauty of education, whether traditional or alternative, is that it's a lifelong journey. But acquiring knowledge is just the first step. The real magic happens when you **apply what you've learned** to real-world scenarios.

3. What to Do with Your New Knowledge

3.1 Applying It in University

Firstly, let's talk about those of you who are currently in university. I get it; university life is a whirlwind of lectures, assignments, and social commitments. And for some of you, there's the added pressure of part-time jobs to cover tuition fees. But here's your opportunity: university is also a time when you have a bit more flexibility in your schedule compared to a 9-to-5 job. So, how can you make the most of this time to apply the knowledge you've gained from alternative educational avenues?

Start by **aligning your coursework with your interests and the skills** you've acquired outside the classroom. If you've been diving into books on entrepreneurship, consider taking business-related electives. If online courses on coding have caught your fancy, look for projects or assignments where you can apply these skills. The key is to create a synergy between your formal education and your self-directed learning journey. This not only enhances your academic performance but also adds a layer of practicality to your theoretical knowledge.

Now, let's talk **about time management**. You might be thinking, *"I'm already swamped with coursework; how can I possibly find time for anything else?"* The answer lies in micro-learning. Break down your learning goals into smaller, manageable tasks. Even dedicating just 20 minutes a day to reading a book or watching an online tutorial can make a significant difference over time. Remember, Rome wasn't built in a day, and neither is your skill set.

When it comes to **coaching** you might be thinking, *"Coaching sounds great, but as a student, I can't afford it"*. Well, many universities offer peer coaching programs where students help students. While this may not be the same level of coaching experience I described earlier, it's a fantastic starting point. Participating in a peer coaching program can not only offer you valuable insights but also make you more coachable down the line. In this context I would also like to talk about your professors. Always remember that you're essentially their client; you're paying for your education. Professors often forget this due to the pressures of publishing and grading, but you're there to learn from them. A subtle yet effective way to remind them of this dynamic is to be an active participant in class. Better yet, volunteer to assist them in their research. This does two things: it builds a personal relationship with your professor, and it often leads to mentorship. By becoming a professor's assistant, you're not just gaining a coach/mentor; you're also applying your skills in a real-world setting and learning new ones along the way.

So, if you're in university, seize this time as an opportunity for holistic growth. Create coherence between your academic pursuits and your self-directed learning while managing your time wisely. This might look challenging but it's all about setting priorities and taking small, consistent steps toward your goals.

3.2 Applying It in the Workforce

For those of you already in the workforce, the challenge of applying new knowledge can seem even more daunting. With a 9-to-5 job, family commitments, and perhaps even a side hustle, your plate is already full. But let's not forget, the busiest people are often the most productive. Why? Because they've mastered the **art of prioritization** and time management. So, how can you, too, apply your newfound knowledge in a busy work environment?

First, let's delve into the importance of continuous learning. In a fast-paced work environment, complacency can easily set in. You might think, *"I've got a stable job; why rock the boat?"* However, in today's rapidly evolving landscape, **skills can become obsolete** almost overnight. Therefore, make learning a daily commitment. Whether it's tuning into a podcast during your commute or dedicating 30 minutes before bed to catch up on industry trends, consistency is key. Small, regular efforts can yield significant long-term benefits.

Next, focus on **identifying gaps** in your current role where your new skills could be an asset. For example, if you've been honing your data analytics skills in your free time, scout for projects at work that could benefit from these insights. The objective is to make your newfound skills visible. **Volunteer for tasks** that allow you to demonstrate these capabilities. This not only enhances your value to the team but also provides a practical avenue for your self-directed learning.

Now, let's pivot to the topic of mentorship and coaching. In a corporate setting, mentors are invaluable. They offer insights to help you navigate office politics, identify growth opportunities, and even advocate for you in matters like promotions or high-profile projects. If your company has a **mentorship program**, seize the opportunity. Otherwise, take the initiative to find a mentor yourself. A competent mentor can offer both professional and personal guidance, aligning your new skills with your career aspirations. Only choose as mentors people who reached what you aspire to accomplish. You need somebody who can give you practical advice. Avoid *"big talks"* who have nothing to back up their advice. A mentor-mentee relationship is in its essence a friendship expressed in a professional setting. So, approach people that are also willing to learn from you, it has to be mutually benefitting.

If your company offers an **internal coaching program**, apply the criteria discussed earlier in the *"how to choose a Coach"* section.

Make sure the coach's skills line up with your goals, gather feedback from colleagues, and schedule a trial session to gauge personality fit. Don't opt for these coaching sessions solely because they're free; you could be using that time more effectively with a coach who can catalyze significant career advancement. If no suitable coaching program exists, consider discussing your coaching aspirations with HR. Persistent negotiation can lead them to (partially) subsidize your coaching sessions.

Speaking of **negotiation**, the term can be daunting, particularly for women who often hesitate to negotiate for promotions or salary increases. However, when it comes to your educational journey, as Chris Voss says: *"Never split the difference"*.[15] If you find negotiation challenging, your learning path serves as an excellent starting point. The stakes are relatively low, and it's a win-win situation: you acquire new skills, and your employer gains a more skilled workforce. Consider this your training ground to sharpen your negotiation skills. During performance reviews for example, seize the opportunity to outline your desired training path. The key is to demonstrate the mutual benefits of the course or training you wish to attend, and to assure your manager that it won't interfere with your work performance or deadlines.

The corporate world may seem like a labyrinth of deadlines and responsibilities, but it's also a playground for applying your new skills. Prioritize your learning, make it visible, and don't shy away from negotiating for what you genuinely believe will benefit your career in the long run.

---

15 Voss, C. (2017) 'Never split the difference'. Cornerstone.

What to remember

- **The Importance of Continuous Learning:** financial prosperity is closely tied to a commitment to continuous learning. A learning mindset is essential for long-term financial success.

- **The Pitfalls of Shortcuts:** shortcuts to wealth, such as "get rich quick" schemes or relying on third-party advisors, are risky and often lead to financial instability.

- **Limitations of Traditional Education:** traditional educational systems often lack practical application and personalization, focusing more on theoretical knowledge that may not be directly applicable in real-world scenarios.

- **The Value of Alternative Learning Paths:** alternative educational avenues like online courses, mentorship programs, and self-study offer practical knowledge essential for financial decision-making.

- **The Power of Reading:** reading is a simple yet effective way to gain knowledge. The "3-book rule" can elevate your understanding of a subject to an "expert amateur" level.

- **Coaching and Seminars:** coaching and seminars provide not just knowledge but also a sense of community and networking opportunities. Understanding the difference between coaching and therapy can help you choose the right path for personal development.

- **Online Education:** the digital landscape has democratized education, offering flexibility and a sense of community. However, due diligence is required to avoid scams or subpar courses.

- **Application in University:** university students can synergize their formal education with self-directed learning for a more holistic educational experience.

- **Application in the Workforce:** those in the workforce should focus on finding opportunities where they can use their new skills at work.

- **Time Management and Prioritization:** both university students and working professionals can benefit from effective time management and prioritization to make room for continuous learning.

CHAPTER 3

My personal journey

Life is always happening FOR you, not TO you.

Tony Robbins

Before we delve into the intricacies of web3 and *blockchain*, I think it's important to pause and share my personal journey with you. Chapters 1 and 2 laid the groundwork for the mindset needed to create wealth and to navigate the crypto universe. Chapter 3 offers a glimpse into the experiences that shaped these beliefs and led me to transform from a little refugee girl to successful entrepreneur and investor. My aim here is twofold. First, I want to demonstrate how the principles I've discussed have been practically applied in my own life. Second, I aim to humanize my story to make it relatable. Success can sometimes create a facade that obscures the real person behind it. I want to show you that no matter where you start, achieving financial success is possible if you approach it methodically. This chapter also sets the stage for upcoming discussions that focus more on *blockchain* and entrepreneurship.

As I touched upon in Chapter 2, I'm a firm advocate for personalized learning paths. So, feel free to read the chapters of this book in any order that suits you. While this chapter provides valuable context, it's not a prerequisite for understanding the chapters that follow. If you find yourself curious or craving more backstory, you can always circle back to this chapter. With that said, let's dive into my personal journey.

1. Childhood

My name is Sanja; in Slavic this means, *"she dreams"*. Before I was born, my mother suffered several miscarriages but never lost sight of her dream to have a baby – and eventually in 1985, I was born, in Sarajevo, the capital of Bosnia and Herzegovina. So Sanja seemed like the perfect name for me and an identity I have embraced because, as you will see, dreaming of a better tomorrow was a necessity for me to get through the challenges I had to face in my early years.

I spent my childhood in Sarajevo until I was five. In 1991, my father received a job opportunity in Italy. Little did we know then that this move might have saved our lives.

At the time, Bosnia and Herzegovina was part of the Socialist Republic of Yugoslavia, and its capital Sarajevo, often referred to as the *"Jerusalem of Europe"*. was known for its long history of cultural and religious diversity. Still today, the city is home to a mosque, Catholic church, Eastern Orthodox Church and synagogue, all within a single neighborhood. No one could have foreseen that this harmonious city would turn into a literal bloodbath. The Bosnian independence declaration in April 1992 marked the beginning of a war that would last four years, claiming nearly 100,000 civilian lives and forcibly displacing over two million people. During this time, Sarajevo's citizens were subjected to daily shelling and sniper attacks, cut off from the rest of the world.

In those early years, I faced the challenges of growing up in a foreign country while living in constant fear for the well-being of my loved ones back home. We witnessed the war's devastation on our TV screens, seeing cities I once thought of as safe and peaceful burn to the ground. My family took in Bosnian refugees fleeing Sarajevo, offering them shelter in our modest two-bedroom apartment in Italy. Although I was safe, I felt the war's pain deeply.

Sadly, not everyone was as fortunate to escape. We had many family members stuck in Bosnia, and communication was scarce. We could only hope they were safe. Eventually, a tunnel was built under Sarajevo, allowing my grandmother and aunt to escape and join us in Italy, where they sought political asylum. My grandfather was less fortunate; he was stuck in the countryside and ended up dying during the war. My cousins were forced out of their home after it was destroyed by bombs. They took refuge in my parents' property, living there for months under conditions that could hardly be called living.

They were frightened, starving, and contemplating suicide as a way out. Sending money was nearly impossible; even when we managed, the equivalent of 1,000€ barely covered the cost of eggs. They used what little money they had to buy alcohol, attempting to numb their unbearable misery. Miraculously, my cousins survived and have since become some of the most successful people I know. Experiencing hunger and oppression yet surviving instilled in them, and in me, a lifelong desire for success.

Like many families, we lost everything; properties were destroyed, and the entire banking system collapsed, all in the name of *"freedom"*. These experiences as a Bosnian refugee ignited my passion for financial inclusion and independence. We're all accustomed to working for an income, paying taxes, and trusting our government and banks to safeguard our well-being. However, the war in Bosnia (and Ukraine recently) has exposed the fragility of these systems, revealing how they can fail us when we need them most.

Thinking of my childhood experience, two distinct feelings come up at the same time.

On one side, my childhood holds some of the most cherished memories of my life. My mum did the best she could with the resources that were available to her. Every summer, we would retreat to our seaside house in Croatia, a place that holds the most beautiful memories of my childhood. This old house, built by my grandfather, was situated on a small island with just about 15 houses in our vicinity. The simplicity of life there was its charm. With no supermarkets or shops nearby, and even devoid of electricity, we lived by candlelight. The absence of modern distractions meant spending quality time with others, playing games, and engaging in heartfelt conversations. Despite its modesty, for me, it was pure bliss.

On the other hand, life in Italy was a stark contrast. I never really felt at home there. First, we were considered an immigrant worker family but suddenly it became worse as they added the refugee stigma onto us. The local children shunned me, refusing to play. My father's presence was sporadic, making him feel like a stranger in our own home. My mother, shouldered the family's responsibilities alone, sacrificing her career to ensure our well-being. She tried her utmost to shield me from the harsh realities, perhaps hoping to protect my innocence. Unfortunately, her silence about the situation inadvertently sowed seeds of fear in my young mind. I grew up under a cloud of insecurities about the future. One of my earliest memories is building a tent in my bedroom, creating a safe space away from the fears and anxieties that engulfed the world around me.

Reflecting on those years, I've come to realize that both these contrasting experiences have shaped me. Despite the challenges, I wouldn't trade my childhood for anything. It's the blend of these memories, both bitter and sweet, that has molded me into the person I am today. Through the lens of coaching, I've learned to reframe these experiences, viewing them not as isolated incidents but as integral parts of my journey, like two sides of the same coin. Coaching has illuminated these memories in a new light, allowing me to appreciate them for the lessons and resilience they've given me.

2. High School Years

My parents seldom discussed the future, and everything about my past and present felt bleak and beyond my control. My father had a tendency for secrecy and would make abrupt, life-altering decisions that left me feeling rootless.

This was most evident when, after the war, he returned to Bosnia to claim an inheritance from my grandfather. Initially, when I was 12, I stayed in Italy in a boarding school, but the uncertainty about what lay ahead consumed me. I developed anorexia as a way to exert some control over my life. Eventually, I was sent back to Bosnia – or what remained of it post-war. Sarajevo, the city of my childhood, lay in ruins. Nothing had been rebuilt; my past was obliterated.

Faced with the hopelessness around us and the lack of opportunities, my parents decided to move to Split, Croatia. This is where I spent my high school years, which were among the most challenging periods of my life, both socially and within my family.

In Split, we lived a somewhat middle-class lifestyle. To outsiders, we appeared to be a picture-perfect family, but the reality was far from it. There was a constant air of secrecy at home. My father, already in his 50s, had stopped working, and we had no clue where our finances stood. We were at his mercy, uncertain if he was wisely investing the money or squandering it. This lack of transparency made me a staunch advocate for female financial independence. I saw first-hand how my mother and I were rendered powerless in this situation. That's why I'm committed to empowering women to take control of their financial destiny. Even today, my husband and I maintain separate bank accounts, and I manage my own finances. This isn't about mistrusting men; it's about women having the skills and mindset to be financially independent and in that way be an independent strong pillar for the family.

Socially, life in Split was a struggle. I was a young, fragile woman with no sense of grounding or self-confidence. My early life had been marked by constant displacement; first as an immigrant in Italy and then an immigrant in Croatia; making me feel perpetually like an outsider. At school, my foreign status made me a prime target for bullies.

My background is a mosaic of cultures: Croatian by origin, born in Bosnia, with a Jewish father and an atheist mother. In Italy, I had been exposed to various ethnicities and even attended a Catholic elementary school. Diversity was my norm. However, in Split, I encountered a society rife with prejudice, especially post-war.

I was constantly ridiculed and questioned about my identity. *"Are you Jewish? Are you Muslim? Are you Croatian?"* These sarcastic questions still haunt me. For many, the memory of their first date is something they can look back on affectionately. This certainly wasn't the case for me. I was asked out by some boy from school, whose name I don't remember. He invited me to go for a drink, the idea seemed fun, worst-case scenario it would be slightly awkward or unmemorable, or so I thought. In fact, the whole thing was a set-up, he only invited me out so that he could taunt me for being *"different"* – all because I was Bosnian, not Croatian. The whole thing was humiliating. This was about the time that I was struggling with an eating disorder, and this only made things worse. To be lured into meeting someone because you believed they were attracted to you, only to find out they were in fact in contempt of you, is an awful experience, particularly for a young girl who had been brought up witnessing her mother get treated badly by her father.

These kind of episodes had long-lasting repercussions, making me see my diverse background as a handicap rather than an asset. It took years for me to embrace my unique heritage. Instead of feeling rootless, I began to see the world as my home. This shift in perspective has been invaluable in my adult life, allowing me to live in various countries and adapt to different cultures. Each new place and experience have enriched my identity, making me a bridge-builder in multicultural settings. This has been particularly beneficial in my role as the CEO of a tech company that employs people from around the globe. My diverse background has enabled me to make diversity in our company not just a slogan but a lived experience.

3. University Years

My identity crisis had left me with a shaky self-image and low confidence. I felt vulnerable, susceptible to being swayed by external forces. I yearned for independence and freedom, and I knew that university would be my ticket to a different life.

Growing up, I was often told that I was too ambitious, a perception deeply rooted in cultural norms. In most Croatian and Bosnian families, women have a clearly defined role: to take care of the family. While they are encouraged to work, their ambitions are often capped at junior positions. My grandmother and mother, however, dared to think differently, and they were considered outliers for it. Why push your daughter to excel, they were asked, when she could simply marry a wealthy man? This cultural backdrop made my school experiences quite unique. When asked about our future aspirations, while most girls spoke of motherhood, I declared, *"I want to change the world for the better"*. It was this unquenchable ambition that fueled my work ethic and ultimately earned me a scholarship to Bocconi University in Italy.

My university years were some of the most fulfilling of my life. The scholarship alleviated financial pressures, allowing me to immerse myself in the social and academic facets of university life. I was fortunate to attend prestigious institutions in Italy and Denmark that provided me with an excellent education, at least on paper. However, upon reflection, I realize that my education had gaps. No one taught me how to create wealth or invest for myself. Entrepreneurship was never presented as an option. The narrative was clear: pursue a career in consulting, investment banking, or a high-tech firm, earn a great salary, and that's the pinnacle of success. This traditional path was so heavily promoted that I, too, found myself walking it down. But as I navigated this route, I couldn't shake off the feeling that there was more to life than what was laid out before me. This period of introspection was the catalyst for my later endeavors, encouraging me to look beyond conventional wisdom and forge my own path. It's a lesson I carry with me to this day: never let societal norms or expectations limit your potential. Your ambition is not a flaw; it's a compass guiding you toward your true north.

4. Early Career

Fresh out of university, armed with a Master's thesis on e-commerce, I was naively convinced that the job market would welcome me with open arms and a hefty pay check. Reality, however, had other plans. Like many others, I found myself navigating the disheartening maze of unpaid or poorly paid internships, all in the quest for that elusive permanent contract.

It was the Vodafone Graduate Program that finally offered me my first taste of corporate life. As I gained experience, my career trajectory began to crystallize. I climbed the corporate ladder, transitioning from one employer to another, eventually landing a role at eBay. There I was, living the so-called dream: a middle-management position in e-commerce, a substantial salary, and life in a vibrant European city. Yet, something felt off.

I couldn't shake the feeling that I was merely a cog in a vast machine designed solely for production and consumption. Despite my passion for my work, its impact felt negligible. Moreover, my earnings seemed to evaporate as quickly as they came in. I was ensnared in a perpetual cycle of earning and spending, largely due to my lack of personal finance skills. In retrospect, I embodied what Robert Kiyosaki describes as a *"poor dad"*, well-educated and gainfully employed, yet woefully lacking in financial literacy and entrepreneurial wisdom.[16]

16 *Kiyosaki, R. T. (2017). 'Rich dad, poor dad' (2nd ed.). Plata Publishing.*

A pivotal moment arrived then in my late twenties when I stumbled upon Tony Robbins' book, *"Master the Game"*, a comprehensive guide to achieving financial freedom through *"seven simple steps"*. Robbins' interviews with successful individuals provided invaluable insights for me about effective money management. My key takeaway? Success in financial matters is largely a question of mindset. Your background, education, or even whether you have a college degree, are secondary. What truly matters is cultivating the right attitude toward money. Also, I learned about the power of compounding: investing consistently, diversifying your portfolio, and adhering to a well-thought-out strategy. If something isn't working, change it; otherwise, stick to your plan. With perseverance and common sense as your allies, success is not just possible – it's probable.

This newfound understanding of finance was a revelation, but the real revelation came when I delved into the world of *cryptocurrency* and *blockchain*. This was not just another financial avenue; it was a revolution, a paradigm shift that promised not just financial freedom but also a chance to make a meaningful impact. And so, armed with a blend of corporate experience and financial literacy, I took my first steps into this exciting new frontier, eager to carve out a space where my work could truly make a difference.

From there I only became more interested in finance which should lead me eventually to hit the jackpot of inspiration – the world of *cryptocurrency* and *blockchain*.

5. Late Corporate Career & Entrepreneurship

In my concluding corporate role at PayPal, my team and I were at the forefront of devising payment solutions for Marketplace players. As I delved deeper into the intricacies of the subject, a glaring issue emerged: the transaction fees for payments were not only high but also lacked transparency. Driven by a desire to streamline payments, I embarked on research to unearth potential solutions. My prior investments in *cryptocurrency* in 2017 led me to realize that *blockchain* technology could be a game-changer. I even identified potential partners and eagerly presented my findings to my managers. However, the timing was premature; there was little appetite for adopting an untested technology that would benefit the client more than PayPal. This experience taught me a valuable lesson: while corporate work is respectable, driving change within such an environment is often a slow and politically fraught process. I felt that familiar tug of dependency, a lack of self-determination, but that was about to change.

During my research, I stumbled upon a white paper from a company called Utrust, which precisely aligned with my vision of leveraging *cryptocurrency* and *blockchain* to solve existing payment issues. Intrigued, I reached out to the founder, Nuno, via LinkedIn. To my surprise, he flew in from Portugal to meet me. Over lunch, our mutual enthusiasm was palpable. What began as a side project gradually consumed more of my time and passion, until I made the audacious decision to leave my well-paying job for this entrepreneurial venture. Many deemed my move reckless, especially those whose lives revolved around job security. However, from a perspective of abundance, letting such an opportunity slip away seemed riskier. Various coaching sessions and seminars had instilled in me the belief that when you're ready, the universe will present opportunities; the challenge lies in recognizing and seizing them. Despite the fear of the unknown, all signs pointed to this being a pivotal moment, a crossroads that required bold action.

To paint an honest picture, the journey wasn't all rosy. It demanded significant sacrifices, including a dip in income, embracing the uncertainty of a new market and facing a lot of rejections, especially at the beginning. Navigating a crypto start-up amidst a global pandemic was no walk in the park. Yet, the learning curve was steep, far surpassing anything I could have gained in a corporate setting. My passion for financial inclusivity found a new home in *cryptocurrency*. Traditional payment companies have yet to fulfil their promise of enabling global trade for all; digital currencies can bridge this gap by empowering people to truly own and instantly spend their money anywhere in the world, while drastically reducing associated costs.

Skeptics may dismiss this technology as a fleeting trend. Yet, the tangible impact of *cryptocurrency* is undeniable but consider for example the Ukrainian war, where over \$135 million in *cryptocurrency* was mobilized to bolster the Ukrainian cause. Having witnessed the ebb and flow of governments, the potential of a currency free from governmental or banking oversight still excites me. My pursuit of greater freedom is at the heart of nearly everything I do, and breaking corporate shackles and accepting the risks of entrepreneurship has made me the happy and successful woman I am today.

CHAPTER 4

Demystifying *Web3* and *Blockchain*

*You never change things by fighting the existing reality.
To change something, build a new model that makes the existing model obsolete.*

Buckminster Fuller

In the first three chapters, we laid the groundwork, focusing on mindset and equipping ourselves with the right tools. As we transition into the more practical aspects of your financial journey, it's essential to grasp how the transformative power of emerging technologies can help you reach your goals.

The journey to financial independence is not just about accumulating wealth, but understanding the avenues through which it flows. *Blockchain* and *Web3* are not just mere buzzwords; they represent the future of finance. As we stand on the verge of this digital evolution, the opportunities for both investors and entrepreneurs are vast. However, as with any financial endeavor, **knowledge is power**. Remember, the golden rule of risk management in investment is never to venture into territories you don't fully understand. Diving headfirst into the world of decentralized finance without a clear understanding is like navigating uncharted waters without a compass.

In this chapter, we'll demystify *Blockchain* and *Web3*, shedding light on their significance and the profound impact they already have on the global financial landscape. The transformative potential of *Web3* extends beyond finance, influencing sectors from healthcare to entertainment, reshaping the way we interact, transact, and trust.

For those already knowledgeable in these technologies, consider this a refresher, a chance to solidify your understanding. But if these terms sound alien to you, fear not. This chapter is designed to bridge the gap between curiosity and comprehension. As we delve deeper, you'll gain the clarity needed to make informed decisions, ensuring that you're not just a passive observer but an active participant in this financial revolution.

1. Web3 & Blockchain

As we embark on this exploration, two terms stand out as flagships of this revolution: **Web3** and **Blockchain**. The internet, as we know it, has undergone significant transformations. From static web pages in Web 1.0 to the interactive platforms of Web 2.0, each phase has brought about monumental shifts in how we communicate, transact, and consume information. Now *Web3*, often referred to as *"Web3.0"*, represents the next evolutionary step of the internet, emphasizing decentralized protocols and platforms. The essence of *Web3* is to challenge the status quo by reducing our reliance on tech behemoths like Google, Meta, or Amazon, and placing the power back into the hands of individual users.

But to truly appreciate the transformative potential of *Web3*, we must journey back in time and understand its predecessors.

1.1 Web 1

Brian Brooks, the CEO of BitFury, captured the essence of the early internet in his speech to the U.S. Congress in December 2021: *"If people remember their original AOL account, it was an ability to look in a curated 'walled garden' at a set of content that was not interactive, but was presented to you on AOL, the way that Time Magazine used to show you the articles they wanted you to see inside of their magazine, just you could see it on a screen".*[17]

This encapsulates the dawn of the internet era, known as Web1.0. Emerging in the 1990s, Web1.0 was the foundational layer of the internet, a vast infrastructure of wires and servers enabling computers to communicate. The U.S. government's ARPANET had sent its

---

17 CNET Highlights. (2021, December 8). 'Watch Crypto expert explain the Blockchain to Congress' [Video]. YouTube. https://www.youtube.com/watch?v=pSTNhBlfV_s

inaugural message back in 1969, but the recognizable form of the web didn't take shape until 1991. With the advent of HTML and URLs, users could navigate between static pages, marking the birth of the *"read-only"* web. This phase of the internet offered a passive experience, it was like flipping through the pages of a magazine, but on a digital screen. This marks its humble beginnings, setting the stage for the dynamic transformations that would follow.

1.2 Web2

Transitioning from the static pages of Web1, the dawn of the 2000s opened the doors into a new era of the internet, often referred to as Web2 or Web 2.0. This phase was characterized by its interactive nature, emphasizing user-generated content and the blossoming of social media platforms. Platforms like Facebook, Twitter, and YouTube became the new town squares, where individuals not only consume content but actively participate in its creation and dissemination. Wikipedia democratized knowledge, and Google transformed the way we sought information.

Yet, as we enjoyed this newfound ability to share, comment, and connect, a more subtle transformation was taking place beneath the surface. The very platforms that empowered us began to harness our data, turning our interactions into commodities. The bait of *"free"* services masked the true cost: our personal data. Companies amassed unprecedented wealth by leveraging this data, tailoring advertisements to our preferences and behaviors. While this era did democratize content creation, giving rise to influencers and the sharing economy, it also centralized power in the hands of a few tech giants.

As the years rolled on, the implications of this centralization became evident. Scandals around data breaches, privacy concerns, and the monopolistic tendencies of these tech behemoths began to surface.

Facebook, or now Meta found itself repeatedly at the center stage of these concerns. This culminated in 2019 when the Federal Trade Commission (FTC) levied a staggering $5 billion fine against the tech giant, the heftiest penalty of its kind to date.[18] The realization that users were, in fact, the product being sold led to growing discomfort and a yearning for change. The promise of Web2, while revolutionary in its own right, seemed to be overshadowed by its pitfalls so many wondered if there could be an alternative.

1.3 *Web3*

Imagine the internet as a vast digital landscape where we can read content, write our own, and now, with *Web3*, truly own and govern parts of it. This isn't just a futuristic concept; it's the next evolutionary step in our online journey. At its core, *Web3* empowers us to be more than mere consumers; it allows us to be stakeholders, shaping the very platforms we use.

To truly grasp the essence of *Web3*, let's journey back to 1991. Visionaries W. Scott Stornetta and Stuart Haber initiated a project that would become the cornerstone of *Web3*: *"the blockchain"*. This was a system designed to stamp digital documents with a unique time signature. However, the world wasn't quite ready for its full potential until 2009.

Amidst the shadows of the 2008 financial crisis, a mysterious figure named Satoshi Nakamoto introduced Bitcoin. But this wasn't just another digital currency. It was a bold statement against the traditional financial systems, a currency that wasn't under the thumb of governments or banks. Built upon the very technology Stornetta and Haber had conceptualized, Bitcoin and the *blockchain*

18 *Reuters. (2023, December 11). US judge to hear Meta privacy dispute with FTC next month. The Economic Times. https://economictimes.indiatimes.com/tech/technology/us-judge-to-hear-meta-privacy-dispute-with-ftc-next-month/ articleshow/105912704.cms*

technology behind it promised a decentralized and transparent financial future, challenging the very foundations of how we perceive and handle money.

But what exactly is *blockchain*? Think of it as a digital ledger, transparent and shared among its users. Every transaction made is recorded in this ledger, and these records, once added, are permanent. They can't be altered or deleted. Now, there are different ways these transactions are verified. In systems like Bitcoin, individuals called *"miners"* solve complex mathematical puzzles to validate and add these transactions, earning rewards for their efforts. This method is called ***"proof of work"***. However, newer systems use a ***"proof of stake"*** approach, where those who hold a stake in the system approve a transaction's authenticity. This method is faster and more energy-efficient. In both scenarios, the details of the transaction are open for all to see, but the identities of those involved remain concealed, represented only by unique digital addresses. This blend of transparency and privacy is one of the many outstanding characteristics of *Web3*.

Now this was a lot of information to take in but what are the implications on relying on this kind of technology? The short answer is that it allows for placing ownership and control firmly in your hands. Let's continue by exploring together how this works, and why is it so revolutionary.

First, we need to understand the core of *Web3*: **trust through technology**. This is a huge deal because you don't need anymore different parties middlemanning when a transaction occurs. In traditional systems we're accustomed to the idea that trust is often established through intermediaries. Think of selling a house for example. Typically, you'd involve a notary, ensuring the transaction is legitimate, but also paying a hefty fee for their services. With *Web3*, this process can be streamlined. Imagine recording this sale on a *blockchain*, a digital ledger that, by its very design, ensures the transaction is permanent and unalterable. No need for middlemen, no exorbitant fees, just a direct, secure exchange between buyer and seller.

But we saw many data breaches in Web2, how can this method be secure you may ask yourself? The answer is the decentralized nature of *Web3*. Instead of relying on a single server or entity, data is spread across numerous servers worldwide. This means even if one server faces issues, your data remains safe and accessible from others. More importantly, this decentralization ensures that no single company or government can lay claim to or control your data. In essence, you truly own your online presence.

The picture starts to get clearer; *Web3's* vision is about redefining online interactions. As Ethereum's Gavin Wood insightfully penned in 2014, *Web3* is about reimagining our online experiences with a *"fundamentally different model for the interactions between parties"*. In this envisioned world, what's meant to be public is shared, what's agreed upon is recorded on a consensus-driven ledger, and what's private remains confidential. All communications are encrypted, identities remain concealed, and trust is mathematically enforced. As Wood aptly summarized, we can't place blind trust in governments or organizations. With *Web3*, we don't have to. Instead, we trust in the robustness and integrity of the technology itself.[19]

As you can see this isn't just another technological upgrade. It's not merely about faster speeds or sleeker interfaces. In some instances, you might even find that certain *Web3* applications are slower or less user-friendly than their Web2 counterparts. The essence of *Web3* lies truly in its transformative approach to power and control. Think about

19 Wood, G. (2023, May 11). 'What Is Web 3? Here's How Future Polkadot Founder Gavin Wood Explained It in 2014'. coindesk.com. https://www.coindesk.com/layer2/2022/01/04/what-is-web-3-heres-how-future-polkadot-founder-gavin-wood-explained-it-in-2014/

your current Web2 online experiences. Haven't we all, at some point, felt a twinge of discomfort knowing our online activities are constantly monitored? Or that our personal data, from the music we listen to, to the posts we like, is being sold to the highest bidder? This has become such a norm that many of us have resigned ourselves to this trade-off: convenience at the cost of privacy.

Web3 challenges this status quo. It asks a fundamental question: Why should a handful of tech giants dictate the terms of our online existence? Why can't we enjoy the marvels of the internet without surrendering our autonomy? *Web3*'s answer is clear: We can, and we should! The technologies and dynamics that have dominated our online lives aren't immutable laws; they are the result of specific technological choices made in the past and we can make new ones.

When diving into the *Web3* ecosystem, you'll encounter a diverse array of projects, each with its unique focus. Yet, they all converge on a shared mission: reshaping the internet's power structures. From cryptocurrencies that challenge traditional financial systems to encrypted messaging that ensures private conversations stay private, from open social networks that prioritize users over profits to decentralized systems that make the internet more resilient and democratic, *Web3* is a collective effort to reclaim the internet.

2. Impact of *Web3*

Building on our understanding of *Web3*'s essence, it's crucial to delve deeper into the tangible effects this transformative wave is already having on our world. After all, recognizing the potential of a revolution is one thing, but witnessing its real-world implications truly brings its significance to life. So, where is *Web3* making its mark?

1. **Finance and Money:** traditional banking and financial systems are undergoing a seismic shift, with decentralized finance (DeFi) leading the charge.

2. **The Tokenized Economy:** beyond just digital currencies, we're seeing assets, both tangible and intangible, being tokenized, creating a new realm of trade and ownership.

3. **Companies:** the very structure and ethos of organizations are evolving, with decentralized autonomous organizations (DAOs) challenging conventional corporate norms.

We'll navigate through these domains, to uncover the profound ways in which *Web3* and *Blockchain* are not just future promises but present realities reshaping our world.

2.1 Finance and Money

In our modern, tech-driven world, many of us can instantly check our bank balance, transfer money, or even invest in stocks with just a few taps on our phones. But here's a reality check: there are about 1.7 billion people out there who can't do any of that. They're completely cut off from the traditional banking system. In places like Sub-Saharan Africa, almost half the population is in this boat, and it's even tougher for women.[20]

I remember this one time when I was in Fiji for a seminar. I took some time to visit the local villages, and what I saw was both eye-opening and heart-wrenching. People there were getting paid in cash, and they'd literally store that cash in their homes. Why? Most of them didn't have something as basic as a passport or an ID. So, opening a

---

20 Klapper, L. (2023, September 18). 'New Findex notes showcase digital financial inclusion in Sub-Saharan Africa'. *World Bank Blogs.* https://blogs.worldbank.org/africacan/new-findex-notes-showcase-digital-financial-inclusion-sub-saharan-africa

bank account is not possible for them.

I wanted to make a difference, even if it was small. I decided to sponsor a kid's education and send some money to their family. But here's the kicker: the only way to get the money to them was through MoneyGram. They'd go there, withdraw the cash, and end up losing a chunk of it, sometimes as much as 10 to 20%, just in fees, which is considerable.

This isn't just a story about Fiji or Africa. It's a global issue. To solve this situation, we need a holistic approach. *Web3* by design provides the opportunity to revolutionize the financial landscape, especially for those who've been sidelined by the traditional system.

2.1.1 Inclusivity

The beauty of *Web3* is its simplicity and inclusivity. Imagine a world where all you need to access and manage your money is a smartphone. With *Web3*, it is a reality! Here's how it works: You simply download a *Web3* wallet onto your smartphone. That's it. No lengthy paperwork, no need for a physical address, and certainly no need for official IDs or passports. Once you have your wallet, you are part of the global *Web3* financial system. You can send and receive money directly from one person to another, anywhere in the world, just by knowing their wallet address. It's peer-to-peer, you and the recipient, cutting out all the middlemen like banks, transfer services or third-party processors that traditionally slow things down and rack up fees. This is why transferring money internationally via *Web3* costs a fraction of what the traditional system charges, adding to the inclusivity aspect of *Web3*.

This democratization of finance means that everyone, regardless of where they live or their socioeconomic status, can participate in the global economy.

2.1.2 Ownership

You might think, like I once did, that you have full control over your hard-earned money. That you can access it, move it, and spend it whenever and wherever you please. But let me share a personal story that shattered this illusion for me.

I was on a trip in a foreign country, equipped with my main credit card from one of the UK's largest banks and a prepaid multi-currency card. I felt prepared. But then, out of the blue, my bank decided to freeze my funds. They suspected fraud when I tried to transfer money from one account to another. The irony? At that time, I was working for PayPal, one of the world's leading payment companies. Here I was, two decades after my company had revolutionized digital payments, stranded in a foreign land, entirely at the mercy of a bank's whims. And while I was relieved it wasn't an actual fraud, it got me thinking: How is it possible that I don't have full control of my money? The answer is simple. When you swipe your credit card or click 'pay' online, there's a whole backstage drama unfolding. Multiple players, from the bank issuing the card, the credit card scheme, to the payment gateway, all have a say in whether your transaction goes through. And if it does, each one takes a cut for their 'service'. It's a deeply convoluted system. This experience underscored for me the importance of truly owning and controlling your funds. And that's where *Web3* and cryptocurrencies come into play. They offer a system where you have genuine ownership. No middlemen, no hidden players pulling the strings. Just you and your money, interacting in a transparent and direct manner.

2.1.3 DeFi

There is a revolutionary concept that's reshaping the financial landscape: DeFi, or Decentralized Finance.

At its core, DeFi is like the financial services you're familiar with, but with a twist. Imagine all the banking and financial services you know: loans, savings, trading, insurance - but without the banks or any central authority. Instead, these services operate on *blockchain* technology, the same underlying technology we discussed earlier. It's again peer-to-peer, transparent, and most importantly, inclusive.

DeFi democratizes finance. For instance, if you need a loan in the traditional system, you'd have to go through a series of background checks, income verifications etc. And sometimes aspects that are not in your power like your ethnicity or neighborhood could influence the decision. But with DeFi, you can approach a decentralized platform, and if you meet the criteria set by the code (like having enough collateral), you get the loan. No questions asked, no biases, just a straightforward transaction.

But it doesn't stop at basic services. For those who are more financially savvy, DeFi offers advanced opportunities. You can leverage your assets to participate in larger transactions, taking on bigger risks for potentially bigger rewards. It's like playing in the big leagues, but the entry ticket is accessible to everyone, not just the elite.

This shift is monumental. With DeFi, the barriers that once excluded many from the world of finance are crumbling. Everyone, regardless of their background or financial status, gets a seat at the table. It's not just a new way to do finance; it's a more inclusive, fair, and transparent one. One could actually say that DeFi creates a paradox: while giving access to people to financial instruments, a growing number of people become *"unbanked"* as DeFi gains traction. DeFi actually changes how we perceive the term *"unbanked"*. Historically, being unbanked was synonymous with financial exclusion, often associated with the marginalized or those in developing regions without access to traditional banking. But today, the narrative is evolving.

As DeFi technology matures and gains traction, the definition of *"unbanked"* is undergoing a profound transformation. It's no longer about those left out of the traditional financial system. Instead, it's becoming a conscious choice for many who are disillusioned with the limitations and biases of conventional banking. They're choosing to step away, to *"unbank"* themselves from a system that, in many ways, has catered to the interests of a select few.

While the transformative potential of DeFi and the broader *Web3* ecosystem is undeniable, it's not without its skeptics. Some dismiss it as a passing trend, while others go as far as labeling it a scam. However, to truly understand the impact and significance of this technology, one needs to look beyond the noise and consider real-world applications.

A compelling testament to the power of crypto and *Web3* is its role during crises, where traditional systems might falter. The recent conflict in Ukraine offers an example where everything we have seen so far about *Web3* comes together to bridge the gap when institutions and traditional financial mechanisms were strained.

Elliptic, a leading *blockchain* analysis company, reported that pro-Ukrainian war efforts amassed donations exceeding $212 million in *cryptocurrency*. Out of this, about $80 million in crypto was directly channeled to the Ukrainian government. These funds have been instrumental in supporting various war-related initiatives, from procuring bulletproof vests, helmets, and demining equipment to essential items like medical supplies and radios. The beauty of cryptocurrencies lies in their speed and efficiency. Donations can be sent swiftly, bypassing the usual bureaucratic hurdles and intermediaries.

Moreover, the decentralized nature of cryptocurrencies allowed individuals to send funds peer-to-peer. Those who recognized the potential of crypto ensured they had a digital wallet, enabling them to receive funds directly.

The war also saw the rise of non-fungible tokens (NFTs) as a means of support. Ukraine DAO, a decentralized autonomous organization, auctioned an NFT of the Ukrainian flag, raising a staggering $6.75 million for the cause.

Reflecting on this, I can't help but think about the Yugoslav war. How different would things have been if *Web3* and cryptocurrencies were available then? A decentralized system, independent of traditional banking, would have empowered individuals to convert their fiat money into crypto, ensuring financial autonomy. Friends and family could have seamlessly sent funds across borders,

Furthermore, the transparent nature of *blockchain* could have ensured that aid reached those who genuinely needed it, bypassing corrupt intermediaries. And in times of economic instability, crypto could have offered a refuge from inflation, providing a stable financial alternative during chaos.

In essence, the evolution from the traditional to the decentralized offers not just financial freedom but also hope, especially during times when hope is most needed.

2.2 The Tokenized economy

Tokenization, the process of converting tangible assets or financial instruments into digital tokens on a *blockchain* network, is rapidly gaining traction. At the heart of this innovative concept lies the previously mentioned *blockchain* technology, providing a secure, decentralized platform for the creation, exchange, and trading of these digital tokens. The potential of tokenization is vast, with the promise to reshape financial markets, democratize investment avenues, and herald a new era in the global economy.

To truly grasp the essence of tokenization, we need to understand the evolution of *blockchain* platforms. While the Bitcoin *blockchain* was primarily designed for peer-to-peer currency transactions, newer *blockchains*, like Ethereum, have expanded the horizons. Launched in 2015, Ethereum stands out not just as a *cryptocurrency* but also as a foundational platform. Through the introduction of smart contracts – self-executing agreements governed by predefined rules – this platform allows for the creation of other cryptocurrencies and a broad spectrum of *decentralized applications (Dapps)* atop its structure. This programmability is what sets Ethereum apart. Moreover, Ethereum's tokenization feature has been a game-changer. It has not only revolutionized crowdfunding through Initial Coin Offerings (ICOs) but also paved the way for the rise of decentralized finance (DeFi) applications.

As Ethereum itself is a global decentralized network, it ensures by design that there is no central authority, offering resistance to censorship while creating transparency and security. With its upgradeable nature, Ethereum ensures it remains adaptive, catering to the evolving needs of its vast user and developer community.

So, what's the grand vision behind tokenization? It's about redefining access and breaking down traditional barriers in the world of investments.

Imagine a world where you could own a digital slice of a vintage car collection, a stake in a vineyard producing fine wines, or even a share of royalties from a classic rock song. This is the transformative power of tokenization. It's like turning tangible assets into digital puzzle pieces, where each piece can be owned, traded, or sold, much like shares in the stock market.

The brilliance of tokenization is its ability to offer micro-ownership. It's akin to dividing a grand mansion into thousands of miniature models and allowing individuals to own a piece of it. Whether you're a college student with a modest savings account or a multinational conglomerate, tokenization ensures that the doors to diverse investment avenues are wide open.

These new possibilities created as you might know in 2022 a totally new 41-billion-dollar market, which had a great impact on fashion, art, gaming and many other industries. If you haven't guessed it yet I'm talking about NFTs.

2.2.1 NFTs

It was a moment that took the world by storm. In 2022, an artist named Beeple made headlines when his digital artwork, represented by an NFT, was auctioned off for a staggering $69 million at Christie's. Suddenly, everyone was asking, *"What are NFTs?"* At its core, an NFT, or Non-Fungible Token, is a unique digital asset stored on a *blockchain*. Unlike cryptocurrencies like Bitcoin or Ethereum, where each coin or token is identical to another, NFTs are distinct. Each one carries specific information that sets it apart from any other, making it *"non-fungible"* or irreplaceable.

To break it down further, imagine you have a special edition trading card. While there might be thousands of the same card in circulation, each one has a unique serial number. This number differentiates your card from all the others. In the world of NFTs, this uniqueness is achieved through metadata, a set of data that describes and gives information about other data. So, even if there are 10,000 digital replicas of an artwork, each NFT associated with those replicas will have its own distinct metadata, making it one-of-a-kind.

Now, let's tackle the term *"fungibility"*. In the financial world, something is considered fungible if it can be exchanged on a one-for-one basis without any loss of value. For instance, if you swap a $10 bill with someone else's $10 bill, neither of you is at a loss. They're interchangeable. But with NFTs, this isn't the case. Each token has its own inherent value based on its uniqueness. It's like trading a signed first edition of a book for a regular print; they aren't of equal value.

The rise of NFTs has opened up a realm of possibilities for artists, musicians, and creators. It's a digital revolution, allowing them to monetize their work in ways previously unimagined. And for collectors, investors, and you NFTs offer a new frontier of unique digital assets to explore and invest in. The world of art and collectibles will never be the same again. Here are some very concrete ways in which NFTs have impacted industries and people's life.

Brands

Brands are using *Web3* and create or enhance communities. Let's take a look at the NBA's Top Shot initiative. Instead of just selling merchandise or tickets, they offered fans something unique: the chance to own *"moments"* from games. Think of a spectacular LeBron James dunk, immortalized and tokenized. It's like the digital evolution of basketball card collecting. And guess what? Fans loved it. Speaking of memorable experiences, let's touch on the NFL and Ticketmaster collaboration. Instead of going the traditional route, they offered fans commemorative NFT tickets for Super Bowl events. Your regular ticket was transformed into a digital keepsake, a unique memento of being part of a significant event. It felt authentic and resonated with fans because it aligned with the excitement of attending a live game.

Now, let's look at some big fashion and sportswear players. Brands like Nike, Adidas, and Under Armour didn't just jump onto the NFT bandwagon; they integrated it into their existing brand ethos. They offered NFTs that had dual purposes: some could be used in virtual worlds to dress up avatars, while others gave owners exclusive rights to real-world products or limited-edition streetwear. Did you know that Adidas made $23 million from NFT sales in just one day? It wasn't just about selling digital tokens; it was about creating a new dimension for their community, complete with its own resale market, reminiscent of the buzz after a limited shoe release.

And then there was McDonald's who instead of auctioning their NFTs to the highest bidder, turned it into a fun engagement activity. Want to win an exclusive McDonald's NFT? Just retweet their announcement. Simple, right? The result? A staggering 85,000 retweets and a whole lot of buzz.

In essence, NFTs aren't just about selling digital assets. For brands, it's an opportunity to engage, to create unique experiences, and to build or enhance communities. They understood their audience and offered them through NFTs something that felt innovative, useful and authentic. And as we've seen, when done right, the possibilities are endless.

Artists & content creators

For artist and content creators NFTs represent a world where they can directly monetize their creations, bypassing traditional gatekeepers like galleries or record labels. That's the promise of NFTs for the creative community.

The digital realm has always been a double-edged sword for artists. On one hand, it offers unparalleled reach and exposure. On the other, digital content can be easily replicated, leading to issues of plagiarism and loss of revenue. Enter NFTs. As mentioned before, they're like digital certificates of authenticity, ensuring that a piece of digital art or content is unique. Even if there are multiple copies.

Now, let's break it down a bit. Think of your favorite song or a digital artwork you adore. In the traditional digital world, these can be copied endlessly, with no real way to determine the original. But with NFTs, each digital item gets its own unique identifier. So, even if there are 5,000 copies of a song or artwork, each one is distinct. It's like having a limited-edition trading card, where each card has its own unique serial number. This not only ensures authenticity but also adds a layer of rarity and value to the digital item.

But the magic doesn't stop there. NFTs also tackle the age-old issue of secondary sales. In the past, if someone resold an artwork or a collectible, the original creator didn't see a dime from that resale. With NFTs, artists can embed royalties into their work, ensuring they get a cut every time their creation changes hands. It's a game-changer, providing artists with a sustainable revenue stream.

Now, let's sprinkle in some real-world success stories to paint a clearer picture. Take Emily Yang for example from New York, Emily Yang, known in the art world as Pplpleasr, faced a series of setbacks. The pandemic led to a rescinded job offer from a renowned tech company. However, Emily's resilience shone through. She began creating art, driven by pure passion. A chance introduction to the crypto world revealed a unique opportunity. The crypto space, while technologically advanced, lacked artistic flair. Emily's 3D animations, tailored for crypto projects, quickly gained traction. Collaborations with events like the NFT Virtual Summit and platforms like Uniswap V3 marked her ascent. But the pinnacle was auctioning her art as NFTs. Pieces like *"Apes Together Strong"* garnered significant sums, solidifying her position in the NFT realm. Beyond personal success, Emily's commitment to the NFT and DeFi communities remains unwavering, with a portion of her earnings channeled back into the ecosystem.

Then there's Shelly Soneja from the Philippines. Her journey in digital art is both inspiring and transformative. The world of NFTs brought her unexpected success. Her debut artwork, minted as an NFT, fetched a sum that might seem modest by global standards but was monumental for an artist from a developing nation. For context, her earnings from a single NFT sale could surpass what many in her country earn in months. Now, as a pivotal figure at Altitude Games, Shelly's NFT project, DJEnerates, has gained significant traction. Her story underscores the transformative power of NFTs, especially for artists from regions where financial empowerment can be life-changing.

Last but not least Alejandra Glez, a young Cuban feminist artist, made history as the first in Cuba to venture into the NFT space. Her success was immediate and profound. Within mere minutes, she earned 3 ETH, equivalent to USD 5,700 at the time. To put this into perspective, the monthly minimum wage in Cuba is approximately USD 20. In a nation where the economy has been battered by the pandemic's impact on tourism, Glez's achievement is monumental.

Her NFT artworks are not just visually captivating but also carry a deep message. Glez's art delves into the tales of femicide victims, migrant women enduring hardships, and those subjected to gender-based violence.[21]

Brands like the NBA or Adidas might have the resources and reach to make a splash in the NFT world, but it's stories like Emily's and Shelly's that truly showcase the democratizing power of NFTs. It's a realm where artists, irrespective of their background or location, can carve a niche for themselves, connect directly with their audience, and reap the rewards of their creativity.

NFTs are not just a trend or a buzzword. They're a revolutionary tool that's reshaping the landscape for artists and content creators, offering them autonomy, financial security, and a platform to truly shine. It creates a true win-win situation: you can support amazing women like Alejandra in their artistic endeavors while investing in assets that can grow in value.

---

21 Tech, N. (2023, April 27). '7 Artists who saw their life change thanks to NFTs'. https://www.nfttech.com/newsroom/7-artists-who-saw-their-life-change-thanks-to-nfts

Metaverse & Gaming

In case you are not familiar with the Metaverse, let me explain. Imagine a vast, interconnected universe of virtual worlds where you can hang out, work, play, and even attend concerts. Now, you might be thinking, *"Haven't we seen this before in games like Fortnite or Minecraft?"* Yes, but there's a twist. These games are what we'd call Web2 metaverses. The new wave, the *Web3* metaverse, has additional features powered by *blockchain* technology and NFTs!

For gamers, this is truly a game-changer. You can now own a unique sword in a game, not just as an in-game item, but as a digital asset which you can sell or trade. With NFTs, gamers can basically own their in-game items, from outfits to weapons. Ownership is not the limit; it's also about monetization. Gamers can sell these items in secondary markets, making their gameplay not just fun but potentially profitable. But the Metaverse goes beyond gaming. It's a digital realm that spans across various platforms and experiences. Think of it as the successor to the internet, a 3D, immersive version of it. And just like the internet changed the way we live and work, the Metaverse promises to do the same, but on a grander scale.

You've probably heard about Mark Zuckerberg's vision of the Metaverse, and while it is ambitious, I believe the true Metaverse will not be held by META but will be built on *Web3*. Why? Because *Web3* offers decentralization. It's a world where users have genuine ownership over their assets, identities, and data. No single entity or company can control it. It's a space where everyone should have a say, and that's the beauty of it. Companies like Decentraland and The Sandbox are already pioneering this space. They've created virtual worlds where through cryptocurrencies and NFTs you can build and monetize structures like casinos and even theme parks. A virtual estate in Decentraland recently sold for over $900,000. Mind-blowing, right? The future of the Metaverse is bright, and it's being built on the principles of decentralization, ownership, and true user empowerment. It's a space where creativity meets technology, and the possibilities are endless.

2.3 Companies

Now that we have a better understanding of the tokenized economy let's zoom into one of its main protagonists: *Web3* businesses. I genuinely believe that *Web3*, with its unique characteristics, is set to revolutionize the way companies operate. And if you're wondering how, let's dive right in!

Remember the days when you'd play a video game and find a bug that just ruined the experience? Or when you hoped for an update that would add a desired feature to your game? We've all been there, grumbling and wishing we could do something about it. Well, with *Web3*, that's becoming a reality. Gamers aren't just players anymore; they're investors and decision-makers. They can invest in the games they love and have a say in how they're run. Again, gaming is only an example, but there is a big shift happening in general from the Web2 world, where businesses often saw their communities as pools of clients to monetize towards *Web3*, in which the community is at the heart of the business. They're not just customers; they're an integral part of the product or service. Take *Utrust*, for example. When we launched our product, we already had an engaged community eager to try it out. It didn't stop there; they shared ideas, promoted the product, and some even joined our team, becoming ambassadors for the brand.

But there's another fascinating aspect of *Web3* businesses that sets them apart: transparency. Unlike traditional businesses that keep their development processes under wraps, *Web3* businesses thrive on openness. They develop in public, sharing their roadmaps, future plans, and even potential features. The focus shifts from guarding secrets from competitors to collaborating with the community. It's an open approach that gives community members the possibility to vote on features, give feedback, and suggest improvements. Through this collaborative effort businesses and their communities work hand-in-hand to create products that truly resonate with end-users.

I would like to emphasize that this community approach also reflects in the attitudes of key figures in the *Web3* space. When I first ventured into the *Web3* realm, one aspect that genuinely stood out to me was its incredible accessibility. It's a world where barriers are surprisingly low. I found it astonishing that I could directly engage with developers, innovators, and even business leaders shaping this space. To put it in perspective, while someone like Mark Zuckerberg would probably never even glance at a message I sent him, in the *Web3* community, I've had meaningful interactions with key figures. It's a refreshing change, where voices, regardless of their stature, are heard and valued.

In essence, *Web3* is redefining the business landscape. It's moving away from top-down decision-making to a more inclusive, community-driven approach. Companies in the *Web3* space are not just providers; they're collaborators, working with their communities in a transparent way to shape the future. If we add to this a totally decentralized approach and a flat hierarchy, you get a DAO.

2.3.1 DAOs

Alright, let's dive a bit deeper into the world of DAOs. A DAO, or Decentralized Autonomous Organization, is an organization powered by *blockchain* technology. Instead of being governed by a hierarchy or a CEO, it's run by rules encoded in smart contracts. This allows it to operate in all transparency without a central authority, and decisions can be made collectively.

Here's a quick rundown of what makes DAOs revolutionary:

- **Democratic Decision-making:** in DAOs, decisions are made collectively. If you hold tokens, you get a say. It's governance by the people, for the people.
- **Crystal Clear Transparency:** everything in a DAO is out in the open. Whether it's financial transactions, voting results, or new proposals, it's all recorded on the *blockchain* for anyone to see. No more backdoor deals or hidden agendas.
- **Power to the Community:** in a DAO, it's the community that drives the direction. Anyone with tokens can pitch ideas, vote, and shape the organization's future. It's like a town hall meeting, but on a global scale.
- **Automated Efficiency:** DAOs operate using smart contracts. These are like automated rulebooks that execute tasks without human intervention.
- **Resourceful and Wise:** DAOs often have a pool of funds or resources. And guess what? How these are used is decided by the community. Whether it's for research, community projects, or investments, it's all based on collective wisdom.
- **Open Doors for All:** DAOs don't have a VIP list. If you have the organization's tokens, you're in. No need to know someone on the inside or get special approval.
- **Adaptable and Ever-evolving:** DAOs aren't set in stone. They can change and adapt. If the community feels a rule isn't working, they can propose changes and vote on them. It's a living, breathing entity that evolves with its members.

Now, to bring this concept to life, let's delve into a real-world example: VitaDAO. VitaDAO's mission revolves around longevity science, aiming to extend human lifespan and enhance overall health.

Here's how they operate:

- **Community Governance:** VitaDAO thrives on its community-driven approach. If you're a VITA token holder, you can submit proposals and vote on a myriad of topics, from research projects to potential collaborations.

- **Crowdfunding for Progress:** VitaDAO gathers funds through methods like token sales. These funds are then directed towards pioneering research in fields like regenerative medicine and aging reversal.

- **Research Project Selection:** have a promising longevity-related project? Pitch it to VitaDAO. The community evaluates these proposals and votes on which ones deserve funding.

- **Token-Powered Influence:** the VITA token isn't just a digital currency; it's your voice in shaping VitaDAO's journey. Token holders can use their assets to vote and influence the organization's trajectory.

- **Collaboration:** VitaDAO prides itself on its collaborative ethos. By uniting experts from diverse fields, they accelerate discoveries and foster knowledge sharing.

DAOs, like VitaDAO, are reshaping the very fabric of what an organization can be, heralding an era of inclusivity, transparency, and democracy. These projects embody a significant shift in collaborative and organizational structures on a global scale. While the potential of DAOs is immense, we must acknowledge that they are still in their nascent stages, with much to learn and refine in the years to come. As we journey forward, watching these projects evolve, I'm convinced that in future DAOs will become foundational to our collective endeavors.

3. Joining the *Web3* wave

In order to support your first steps in this new frontier I've crafted a step-by-step guide into the *Web3* world. Take this guide for what it is intended to be, a first step. More guidance on how to navigate this space will follow in the next chapters.

Step 1 - Dive Deep into *Web3* Education

Let's start off with the most fundamental step: educating yourself. Now, I can't stress this enough: if you're serious about riding the *Web3* wave, you've got to be willing to put in the work. This isn't a realm where you can just dip your toes in and expect to surf like a pro. If you're not ready to invest time and effort into understanding this space, then, this book, and perhaps the entire *Web3* world, might not be for you.

Start with the basics. Get a firm grasp on *blockchain* technology and *cryptocurrency*. Familiarize yourself with key concepts. This chapter gave you a brief overview but there is so much more to discover. The internet is full with resources that can help you, but it's essential to filter out the noise and focus on reputable sources. Here are some places to kickstart your journey:

- ***Cryptocurrency* Exchanges:** platforms like Coinbase, and Kraken aren't just for trading. They offer a treasure of educational materials, beginner's guides, blog posts, and tutorials.

- **Online Publications:** stay updated with crypto-centric publications like CoinDesk, CoinMarketCap, Cointelegraph, and Decrypt. Their articles, analyses, and news pieces can be invaluable.

- **Influential Blogs:** some of the brightest minds in crypto maintain personal blogs. For deep dives, check out blogs by industry leaders like Vitalik Buterin (Ethereum's founder), Gavin Wood (Ethereum's co-founder), and Andreas Antonopoulos.

- **YouTube Channels:** if you're more of a visual learner, YouTube has many channels dedicated to crypto education. They offer tutorials, market analyses, and even interviews with industry experts.

- **Podcasts:** for those always on the move, podcasts can be interesting. Tune into shows like *"Unchained"* by Laura Shin, *"The Pomp Podcast"* by Anthony Pompliano or *"The Money Movement"* by Jeremy Allaire for insightful discussions.

- **Online Communities:** engage with fellow enthusiasts on platforms like BitcoinTalk, Reddit's *r/CryptoCurrency*, and various Telegram or Discord groups. These communities are buzzing with discussions, debates, and the latest trends.

- **Crypto Twitter:** the crypto Twitterverse is vibrant and dynamic. Follow influential figures like Vitalik Buterin (@VitalikButerin) for real-time updates and insights.

Remember, as you navigate this vast ocean of information, always approach with a critical mind. Verify facts from multiple sources, stay updated with the latest trends, and never hesitate to ask questions. The *Web3* community is vast, and there's always someone willing to help.

Step 2 - Setting Up Your Digital Wallet

Alright, now that you've got a grasp on the basics, it's time to get hands-on. Think of your digital wallet as your passport to the *Web3* world. It's where you'll store, manage, and secure your cryptocurrencies. But here's the thing: not all wallets are created equal. Let's break it down.

There are primarily two types of wallets: software wallets and hardware wallets. Software wallets like Metamask can be on your mobile, desktop, or even web-based. They're convenient, sure, but if you're looking for more security, you'll want to lean towards hardware wallets. Devices like Ledger are the gold standard here because they give you:

- **Offline Storage:** one of the standout features of hardware wallets is that they store your private keys offline. This means they're out of reach from the vast world of online threats, be it malware, phishing attacks, or those pesky keyloggers.

- **Secure Chip:** these wallets come equipped with a secure chip designed specifically to safeguard your private keys and handle cryptographic operations. It's built to resist any physical tampering, making it a tough nut to crack for any potential attackers.

- **Private Key Generation:** when you set up a hardware wallet, it generates and stores the private keys right within the device. This means there's no need to expose your keys to other devices that might be compromised.

- **Transaction Signing:** here's the cool part. When you make a transaction, the signing happens within the wallet itself. Your private keys? They never leave the device. It's like having a personal banker who ensures every transaction is legit.

- **Backup and Recovery:** life happens. Devices get lost or damaged. But with hardware wallets, you get a recovery seed phrase. It's like a magic spell that can restore access to your funds. But remember, it's crucial to keep this seed phrase safe and away from prying eyes.

- **User Verification:** many hardware wallets come with built-in screens and buttons. This lets you verify and confirm transactions right on the device, giving you full control and peace of mind.

- **Updates:** transparency is key in the crypto world. Many hardware wallets are open-source, meaning their inner workings are out there for the community to scrutinize, ensuring any potential vulnerabilities are spotted and fixed.

In a nutshell, setting up a secure digital wallet is like building a vault for your digital treasures. It might seem a tad overwhelming at first, but trust me, the peace of mind it offers is worth every bit of effort. So, take your time, choose wisely, and remember: in the world of crypto, security is paramount.

Step 3 - Acquiring Your First *Cryptocurrency*

With your digital wallet set up, you're now ready to acquire some *cryptocurrency*. Let's use Coinbase as our go-to exchange for this step. Coinbase is one of the world's largest and most reputable *cryptocurrency* exchanges. It's user-friendly, secure, and offers a wide range of cryptocurrencies to choose from. Here's a brief on how to go about it:

- **Sign Up:** head over to Coinbase's website and sign up for an account. Follow the prompts, set a strong password, and ensure you have access to the email you use.

- **Verification:** coinbase will ask you to verify your identity. This is a standard procedure called Know Your Customer (KYC). It's a security measure to prevent fraud and ensure the safety of all users.

- **Deposit Funds:** once verified, you can deposit your local currency into Coinbase. This will be the money you use to buy your first *cryptocurrency*.

- **Purchase *Cryptocurrency*:** navigate to the trading section and purchase a *cryptocurrency* of your choice. Given that you're just starting, I'd recommend starting with a well-known one like Ethereum (ETH).

As you can see here it's a very straightforward process. I would like to add here a little advice: Start small. Really small. Think of this as your exploratory phase. You're learning the basics, understanding how transactions work, and getting a feel for the space. Maybe you'll use this *cryptocurrency* to pay minor transaction fees, or perhaps dabble in tiny investments. The point is to interact and understand, not to go all in because everyone makes beginner mistakes. Maybe you'll send funds to the wrong address or perhaps misjudge a transaction fee. It happens to the best of us. And the less money you have in play, the less painful these beginner blunders will be.

Remember, the *Web3* world is vast and intricate. It's not just about making big bucks; it's about understanding a revolutionary technology. So, take baby steps and learn from each interaction.

Step 4 - Engage and Connect in the *Web3* Community

The world of *Web3* is vast, and while the technology is a significant part of it, the heart and soul of this movement are its people. The community is where the magic happens. It's where ideas are exchanged, collaborations are forged, and the future of decentralized technology is shaped.

When you dive into the *Web3* space, you'll quickly realize that it's a melting pot of enthusiasts, developers, artists, and visionaries. And the best way to truly understand and be a part of this revolution is to immerse yourself in its community. Engaging in online forums can offer a wealth of knowledge. Platforms like Discord and Reddit are buzzing hubs of *Web3* discussions, where you can ask questions, share insights, or simply lurk and learn. Virtual meetups, webinars, and even in-person events offer a chance to connect with like-minded individuals. These gatherings can be a treasure of information, where you can hear from experts, see what's trending, and even find potential collaborators for your next big idea.

And let's again not forget about Twitter (or X), which has evolved into a significant platform for *Web3* discussions. It's where you can follow thought leaders, get real-time updates, and even participate in enlightening debates.

In essence, the *Web3* community is a vibrant and welcoming space. By actively participating, you not only stay updated on the latest trends but also become a part of a movement that's shaping the future of the internet.

Step 5 - Enter the World of DApps

DApps, or decentralized applications, are the beating heart of the *Web3* ecosystem. Think of them as apps on your phone, but backed by *blockchain*. They're transparent, tamper-proof, and operate without a central authority. And the best part? There's a DApp for almost everything!

Start your journey at platforms like DappRadar. It's like an app store but for DApps. Here, you can get an overview of the most popular and trending decentralized applications across various *blockchains*. It's a fantastic place to discover new DApps, see user reviews, and even track the volume of transactions.

Now, when most people hear DApps, they often think of finance or NFT platforms. And while it's true that DeFi (Decentralized Finance) apps and NFT marketplaces are making waves, the DApp universe is vast and diverse. There are decentralized social media platforms, marketplaces, and even decentralized versions of your favorite productivity tools.

As you begin to explore, remember to interact with a few DApps. Maybe start with something familiar, like a game or a social platform. As you get the hang of it, venture into DeFi or try your hand at an NFT platform. The experience will give you a firsthand understanding of how these platforms operate and the unique features they offer.

The bottom line is that DApps are reshaping our digital world, offering more control, transparency, and opportunities for users. So, take a leap, explore, and immerse yourself in the myriad of possibilities that DApps present in the *Web3* universe.

4. Conclusion

As we wrap up Chapter 4, it's essential to reflect on the transformative journey *Web3* offers. This decentralized frontier isn't just about technology; it's a movement that challenges traditional power structures and offers a more inclusive, democratic, and transparent digital future. By understanding and engaging with *Web3*, you're not only equipping yourself with the tools for financial freedom but also participating in a revolution that prioritizes individual empowerment over centralized control.

However, with great power comes great responsibility. As you venture into this space, remember that you're in full control of your assets. The decentralized nature of *Web3* means that while the rewards can be substantial, the risks are equally significant. If you succeed, you reap the entire benefit, but if you make a mistake, there's no centralized entity to turn to for help. Your funds, once lost, might be irretrievable.

For you, *Web3* can be a golden once in a generation opportunity. You're stepping into a nascent space brimming with supportive individuals, where all doors are still wide open. Whether it's DeFi, NFTs, or other innovations, the tools and platforms available can be your catalysts for growth. And as you thrive, remember that your participation doesn't just enrich you. By supporting artists, developers, and other creators, you're also uplifting others, fostering a community where everyone can prosper together.

What to remember

- **Web3 Revolution:** *Web3* isn't just a technological advancement; it's a paradigm shift that challenges traditional centralized systems. By embracing Web3, you're joining a movement that promotes transparency, inclusivity, and individual empowerment in the digital realm.

- **Educate Before You Dive:** before diving into *Web3*, it's crucial to educate yourself. Understand the foundational concepts like blockchain technology, decentralized networks, and cryptocurrencies. Utilize resources like online courses, blogs, and community forums to build a solid knowledge base.

- **Your Key to *Web3* - Digital Wallet:** setting up a secure digital wallet is paramount. While there are various forms, hardware wallets like Ledger and Trezor offer the most security. They store your private keys offline, ensuring they're shielded from potential online threats.

- **Community Engagement:** *Web3* is as much about the community as it is about technology. Engage in online forums, attend virtual meetups, and connect with like-minded individuals on platforms like Discord and Reddit. This not only keeps you updated but also helps in building valuable connections.

- **DApps - The *Web3* Playground:** dive into the world of decentralized applications (DApps). Platforms like DappRadar offer insights into various DApps, ranging from finance to gaming. Engaging with these applications provides hands-on experience and a deeper understanding of *Web3's* potential.

- **Empowerment and Responsibility:** *Web3* provides tools for financial freedom and offers a space where all doors are open. However, with this empowerment comes responsibility. You're in full control of your assets, so make careful moves.

CHAPTER 5

Unveiling the future: a glimpse into the potential of Web3

By the end of the decade there will be two kinds of companies: (1)Those who fully utilize AI; and, (2)Those who are Out of Business.

Peter Diamandis

Drawing from our understanding of *blockchain* and *Web3*, let us embark on a journey into the horizon of possibilities. As we witness the dawn of this digital revolution, I invite you to envision the next decade with me. I've got my own thoughts on how *Web3* and *Blockchain* might shape our lives, and I'm eager to share them with you. While a portion of this vision might be speculative, it is firmly shaped by current trends, data, and research.

Looking ahead to the next ten years, it's clear that Artificial Intelligence (AI) will be a key player in shaping our future. As this book delves into *Web3* and *Blockchain*, it's crucial to recognize how AI complements and enhances these areas. The combination of AI with *Web3* has the potential to revolutionize not just individual sectors but the very way we think about technology and work. To fully grasp this potential, I'll start this chapter by explaining what AI is. Then, we'll explore how AI and *Web3* can transform different industries.

Ultimately, while I offer my viewpoint as groundwork, remember, you have to craft a personal informed perspective on where this entire domain might lead. Consider this chapter a cornerstone of inspiration, but also a reminder of the ethos of this book: do your due diligence, cross-check my insights with your research, and draw your own informed conclusions.

1. What is Artificial Intelligence

Artificial Intelligence, commonly known as AI, is the branch of computer science that, since the 1950s, has aimed to imbue machines with the ability to perform tasks that would typically require human intellect. These tasks range from understanding spoken words to recognizing faces, solving complex problems, and even creating art or music. It's a technology that's rapidly advancing and weaving itself into the fabric of daily life. Its economic influence is equally significant, with projections suggesting a massive boost to global GDP by 2030, thanks to AI-driven growth.[22]

One of the key components of AI is machine learning, which allows these systems to learn from data. By identifying patterns and applying them to make predictions or decisions, AI systems continuously improve, becoming more effective the more they are used. This learning can be supervised, with humans providing feedback on the AI's performance, or unsupervised, with the AI refining its own algorithms through trial and error, much like how we might learn to play a game better with practice.

With the launch of generative platforms like ChatGPT by OpenAI, public familiarity with AI has surged beyond the speculative realms of science fiction. AI is now a reality, with practical applications that range from chatbots handling customer service inquiries to complex algorithms managing stock trading. As AI continues to evolve, it promises to unlock new potential in every field it touches, all while challenging us to rethink the role of technology in our lives.

1.1 Challenges, limitations and concerns around AI

AI's algorithms aren't working in a vacuum, they are a reflection of the world it learns from: our world. So, when we feed it data, we're also feeding it our biases, and this can be harmful for minorities but also for women in general. I invite you to do a simple image search online to illustrate what I mean: Open your web browser and a search engine like Google or Bing. Go to the image search mode. Type in *"school girl"*, and you'll likely be confronted with sexualized images (especially if your safe-search mode is turned off). Now look for *"school boy"*, and you will be shocked by the contrasting innocence of the results.

---

22 'Impact of artificial intelligence (AI) on the economy & jobs'. (n.d.). Bank of America. https://business.bofa.com/en-us/content/economic-impact-of-ai.html#:~:text=Together%2C%20China%20and%20North%20America,of%20North%20America%20by%2014.5%25.&text=4-,%E2%80%9CUntil%20now%2C%20AI%20could%20read%20and%20write%2C%20but%20not,That's%20rapidly%20changing.%E2%80%9D

This isn't by chance; it's a digital mirror of our society's gender biases, which search engine AIs reflect back to us.

It's examples like this one that make me, even as an AI enthusiast, recognize the concerns that come with rapid AI development. Some experts are ringing alarm bells, going as far as suggesting we might need to hit pause on AI research[23], fearing its potential to accelerate cyberattacks, or, in a more dystopian view, lead to humanity's obsolescence. Even as we debate these scenarios, there are more down-to-earth issues at hand:

- The potential for AI to amplify discrimination, for instance, influencing critical decisions like loan approvals.

- AI's appetite for energy could become a real issue. By 2027, AI could be consuming as much electricity as entire nations[24].

- The possibility of future job displacements. The advent of AI brings a dual impact on jobs: the automation of monotonous tasks and the creation of new career opportunities through and around AI. To bridge this transition, massive skill development and training will be essential for future job readiness.

In the midst of these cultural and regulatory discussions, fear often takes center stage. Will AI replace us? Diminish our creativity? The narrative can get quite grim. But in reality, like with any major technological revolution, where there is disruption on one side, there is creation on the other. Like during the Industrial Revolution, many people lost their jobs as machines replaced them, but it also created many new jobs in the new factories. The question around AI is not whether it is good or bad, but how do we use it? Let's not forget that as humans, we're not flawless. We struggle with complexity and tend

23 'Future of Life Institute'. (2023, November 27). 'Pause Giant AI Experiments: An Open Letter - Future of Life' Institute. https://futureoflife.org/open-letter/pause-giant-ai-experiments/
24 Erdenesanaa, D. (2023, October 11). 'A.I. could soon need as much electricity as an entire country'. The New York Times. https://www.nytimes.com/2023/10/10/climate/ai-could-soon-need-as-much-electricity-as-an-entire-country.html

to make biased decisions based on our limited set of information; that's exactly where we can leverage AI, as a partner to address our shortcomings and tackle the challenges that seem insurmountable alone. I'm not here to tell you those fears are unfounded, but as an AI optimist, I believe in focusing our energy on how AI can collaborate with us to build a better future.

2. Blockchain&WEB3 and AI, a match made in heaven

Now that we have an idea of the potential of both *Web3* and AI, we can take a look at the synergetic potential that they hold together. From my perspective, it's a match made in digital heaven, where the whole is greater than the sum of its parts; a symbiotic relationship that holds the promise of tackling some of the most stubborn problems known to humanity.

Web3, with its decentralized ethos, could ensure that the power of AI doesn't rest in the hands of a few but is dispersed across a vast network, fueling a system that is as fair as it is intelligent. Imagine a DAO where *blockchain*'s transparency meets AI's sharp decision-making. For instance, visualize a *"Clean Ocean DAO"*, born from the union of environmental groups, marine biologists, and concerned citizens. Here, AI doesn't lead but collaborates. It analyzes oceanic data to predict pollution patterns, while *blockchain* ensures every decision and transaction is accountable and transparent. The AI proposes clean-up initiatives based on real-time data and predictive models, while the human collective guides, adjusts, and gives the final nod, ensuring that the heart of the mission, the ocean's health, is always the priority.

This is the crux of the synergy between AI and *Web3*: a dance of calculated suggestions and human-centric governance. It's about leveraging AI's strengths in data analysis and operational efficiency while using *Web3*'s capabilities to coordinate complex, decentralized efforts seamlessly and securely.

To make what I've said here more tangible, we will take a look at different sectors and fields of application to see how *Blockchain* and *Web3* can, individually or together, revolutionize industries.

2.1 Finance and DeFi: Redefining Money Management

We have touched upon the revolutionary nature of Decentralized Finance (DeFi) and its potential to empower individuals financially in the previous chapter. Let's delve deeper into how AI can enhance DeFi to create a more inclusive and efficient financial ecosystem, especially for those traditionally underserved by conventional banking systems.

I envision a future where AI amplifies the power of DeFi by infusing the system with intelligence, creating financial services tailored to the individual user. AI's predictive prowess could enable automated, personalized investment advice, thus democratizing wealth management services that are currently the privilege of the affluent. The advice could also be tailored to one's values, thereby making investments more ethical and contributing to a more sustainable global economy.

Furthermore, imagine DeFi platforms that leverage AI to customize financial products to the unique risk profile of each user, making sophisticated financial strategies accessible to the novice investor and providing a safeguard against beginner mistakes and the volatility of the crypto markets. Now you can expand this vision to include AI-driven tools on these platforms that not only craft a customized investment portfolio but also manage it autonomously, adjusting asset allocation in real time based on sophisticated market prediction algorithms.

AI can also make even more dynamic the already revolutionized processes like loan approvals. Remember when I explained that the entire loan process has been simplified in DeFi by cutting out the middlemen and replacing them with smart contracts? Imagine a future where smart contracts on the *blockchain* not only execute agreements based on pre-programmed conditions but also incorporate an AI's constant risk analysis and input.

Such innovation would make the complex world of decentralized finance more accessible, empowering users to make informed decisions with the help of AI's intelligent analysis, ensuring that both seasoned investors and newcomers can confidently navigate the ebb and flow of the market. In summary, according to me, the future of finance lies in the collaboration between AI and DeFi. By building on this synergy, we can create a financial world where everyone can have a personal financial advisor and thus has a seat at the table.

2.2 Transportation and Travel: Navigating the Future

In the realms of transportation and travel, AI and *Blockchain* are reshaping the journey, bringing unprecedented levels of efficiency, safety, and convenience.

AI will be the **navigator in tomorrow's vehicles**, guiding autonomous cars through the intricacies of traffic with the ease of an experienced pilot. These self-driving vehicles will be able to process environmental data, making decisions in the blink of an eye to ensure passenger safety. The Tesla brand, for example, is already synonymous with this AI-driven future, offering a glimpse of a world where our cars are not just transport, but intelligent companions on the road.

Beyond the car, AI excels in **traffic management**. It will analyze streams of real-time data from a network of sensors and cameras, easing congestion and smoothing out the flow of traffic. The result? Quicker commutes, fewer accidents, and a cleaner environment due to reduced emissions.

Blockchain technology, on the other hand, is the ledger that brings trust. **Decentralized ride-sharing services** will emerge, allowing for direct peer-to-peer interactions without the need for central authorities like Uber. In this way, costs are cut, and trust and efficiency increase. When it comes to **travel**, *Blockchain* has the potential to simplify ticketing and payments, creating a smooth, secure process that transcends borders. It will support validating identities without sacrificing privacy, making check-ins and border crossings hassle-free. *Blockchain*-based loyalty programs can reward travelers in a transparent, easily redeemable manner, fostering brand loyalty and enhancing the travel experience.

In the vast web of **logistics and supply chains**, *Blockchain* ensures that every package, every container, can be tracked with unerring accuracy, securing the supply lines that underpin global commerce.

Now, let's envision a future where AI and *Blockchain* work in tandem. Autonomous vehicles become even safer as *Blockchain* provides a tamper-proof record of maintenance, travel history, and software updates. Traffic flow optimization is not just reactive but predictive, with AI forecasting and *Blockchain* recording and verifying the data.

Imagine smart contracts applied to every aspect of travel; from booking flights to securing accommodations to settling insurance claims. These self-executing agreements on the *Blockchain* can ensure that your trip is protected against unforeseen events, with refunds and claims processed quickly and without dispute. This will lead to decentralized AI powered travel marketplaces which can connect travelers directly with service providers, eliminating intermediaries and reducing costs. AI-driven recommendation systems on these platforms will be able to match travelers with tailored services based on their preferences and past experiences.

I believe that in the future we'll see a travel industry that caters to the needs of its customers like never before. A world where the stress of planning gives way to the joy of experiencing, where travelers have more control over their journeys, and where service providers operate with greater transparency and accountability.

2.3 Health care

In the healthcare industry, the potential of AI and *Blockchain* to enhance patient care and operational efficiency is immense. Individually, these technologies offer significant benefits.

AI provides the predictive analytics necessary for early diagnosis and personalized care. Already, it excels at medical imaging interpretation, where it is as efficient as a trained doctor at detecting anomalies[25]. By serving as a powerful ally in precision medicine, where it can sift through vast amounts of genetic data and patient histories to tailor treatments, AI shows its potential to enhance productivity and accuracy of existing jobs rather than replacing them. This support means a future where medical professionals are equipped with AI tools to keep them up to date of the latest research, allowing more efficient diagnoses and informed decisions.

On the other hand, *Blockchain* ensures the integrity and privacy of health records by offering a reliable and unchangeable record of medical data. This means a patient's health history can be securely shared, fostering a cooperative approach to treatment. The privacy and security of patient information are paramount, and *Blockchain* can manage this data, giving patients control over who has access to their records.

---

25 *King's College London. (2023, December 11). 'AI trained on X-rays can diagnose medical issues as accurately as doctors'. King's College London'. https://www.kcl.ac.uk/news/ai-trained-on-x-rays-can-diagnose-medical-issues-as-accurately-as-doctors#:~:text=11%20December%202023-,AI%20trained%20on%20X%2Drays%20can%20diag-nose,issues%20as%20accurately%20as%20doctors&text=A%20collaborative%20study%20between%20Warwick,or%20more%2C%20accurately%20than%20doctors.*

Let's now take a look together at how both technologies can impact different areas of the healthcare industry.

In the hospital setting, AI could optimize operational efficiency, managing everything from patient admission schedules to supply chains for medical equipment. We have all heard stories of the pressure that medical staff are exposed to and how, out of the resulting stress and fatigue, they can make mistakes with devastating consequences for patients. AI can assist them by automating many of the administrative tasks and obligations, freeing up time to focus on patient care. ***Blockchain***, on the other hand, ensures that all transactions, whether they're updates to a patient's record or the administration of medication, are transparent and permanent. This also allows the patient to better keep track of their treatment and ask informed questions.

In clinical research, AI's role in identifying patterns will expand. Its ability to analyze and interpret vast amounts of complex medical data will give researchers deeper insights and boost the capabilities of physicians. Consider the sheer volume of biomedical papers published each week across the globe, it's an overwhelming amount that no doctor could possibly digest. AI-based tools will bridge this gap, synthesizing and condensing information to provide doctors with daily, actionable insights from the latest research and clinical guidelines. *Blockchain* will authenticate the data's source and ensure its proper use.
Web3 will allow the creation of research DAOs, enhancing collaboration amongst a vast number of researchers. Together *Blockchain*, *Web3* and AI can greatly expedite the research process, paving the way for faster breakthroughs in medicine.

As you can see, AI and *Web3* will contribute in crafting a patient-centered healthcare system that's efficient, secure, and trustworthy.

Healthcare providers will be empowered with tools that enhance their decision-making abilities and ensuring patients' rights and privacy are upheld. As this technology duo matures, we can expect a healthcare landscape that's more responsive to individual needs, where data-driven care becomes the norm, and the security of personal health information is guaranteed.

2.4 Education: The Classroom of Tomorrow

Bringing AI and *Blockchain&Web3* together in education means a synergy that personalizes learning (thanks to AI) and certifies it (through *Blockchain*) in ways previously unimagined. AI will adaptively guide students through a curriculum, while *Blockchain* provides a lasting, verifiable record of their accomplishments.

That being said, I would like to start this exploration by talking about the classroom of the future. By 2030, I envision a world where the Metaverse redefines the concept of the classroom. Accessing a lecture could be as seamless as opening a *Web3* wallet. This could be a game-changer for those unable to travel. For brilliant minds in developing nations, often hindered by restrictive visa policies, the Metaverse promises degrees from world-class institutions at their fingertips. It also offers flexibility for those seeking to balance education with other life commitments. Take parental leave, for instance. Amidst the emotional roller coaster that accompanies the arrival of a new child, many parents experience a sense of isolation or fall into a monotonous routine, especially during extended leaves. The Metaverse could provide a transformative solution, allowing parents to delve into subjects they've always been passionate about from the comfort of their homes, all while cherishing precious moments with their newborns. In the Metaverse, the world's best educational experiences are not bound by geography.

AI in education will be like having a personal tutor for every student, one that understands their unique learning style and pace. Adaptive learning platforms harness AI to customize content, ensuring students aren't left behind or held back by the class average. Intelligent tutoring systems can provide the one-on-one interaction that educators may not always have the bandwidth to offer, catering to each student's needs with precision and patience. This isn't a distant dream, platforms like Duolingo are already personalizing education with AI, proving that efficient learning can be widely accessible. Moreover, educators will benefit from these developments. Imagine the tedious task of grading being streamlined by machine learning algorithms, affording teachers more time to engage with students creatively and personally.

Blockchain in education is equally transformative. It can securely store and verify credentials, turning a once bumpy process into a seamless one. With *Blockchain*, students can carry a lifelong portfolio of credentials, from kindergarten doodles to doctoral theses, in a single digital wallet. Furthermore, the future of learning could well be tokenized, with *Blockchain* facilitating micropayments that allow learners to access and pay for content on their terms. Peer-to-peer learning platforms will create communities where knowledge is shared freely and securely, and smart contracts can safeguard the rights of content creators, ensuring that those who educate are fairly compensated.

The combined power of AI and *Blockchain* in education means a more equitable learning field, where access to quality education is democratized, and where learners are empowered to take charge of their educational journey. The roles of educators evolve, too – they become facilitators and mentors, guiding students through a world where learning is as boundless as their curiosity. As we chart this course, it's vital to mention that technology is not here to replace the traditional classroom but to complement and enrich it.

3. Conclusion

Wrapping up, we're looking at a future packed with opportunities thanks to AI and *Blockchain*. It's clear that while we have some interesting uses now, many of the big changes are still on the way. Whatever the future holds, we've got to use these tools wisely, remembering they're powerful and full of potential, but not without their own set of challenges. As we step into this new space, remember, it's super important to do your own digging, stay curious, and keep learning. This chapter is just the start – your own research is what will really prepare you for what will come next.

What to remember

- **AI & Web3:** the integration of Artificial Intelligence (AI) with Web3 technologies represents a synergistic relationship that could address some of humanity's most persistent challenges, offering a decentralized and intelligent approach to problem-solving.

- **AI:** AI's rapid development in areas such as machine learning, problem-solving, and creative endeavors like art and music is pivotal for the technological advancement that will shape our future, with significant economic impacts predicted.

- **The Double-Edged Sword of AI:** while AI brings enormous potential, it also mirrors societal biases and poses ethical considerations. The key is not to view AI as inherently good or bad but to focus on responsible and equitable use.

- **Empowering the Financial Sphere:** AI will enhance Decentralized Finance (DeFi) by providing personalized, intelligent financial services and advice, while

Blockchain will safeguard the integrity
of financial transactions and democratize
investment opportunities.

- **Transportation:** in transportation, AI's role as a navigator for autonomous vehicles and traffic management will be complemented by Blockchain's trust and transparency in ride-sharing services and logistics.

- **Health Care:** AI and Blockchain will revolutionize healthcare by improving diagnostics and personalized treatments and ensuring the security and privacy of health records.

- **Education Reimagined:** the convergence of AI and Blockchain in education will personalize and certify learning experiences, making quality education more accessible and verifiable.

CHAPTER 6

Identifying opportunities in Web3: investing in the Bitcoin economy

The most important quality for an investor is temperament, and not intellect.

Warren Buffett

After our journey into the future and its possibilities, it's time to anchor ourselves back in the present. The goal of peering ahead was not to indulge in speculation but to identify promising investment opportunities within the *Web3* landscape. Whether you've zeroed in on one of the industries I've spotlighted or discovered alternative avenues, the crucial next step is to understand how to make those investments a reality.

This chapter is a practical guide, crafted to assist you in actively investing within the Bitcoin economy. It aims to equip you with the knowledge to uncover opportunities that align with your investment strategy. In the realm of *blockchain* and *Web3*, you're mainly looking at two investment avenues: NFTs and cryptocurrencies. We'll start by outlining a due diligence process applicable to both NFTs and cryptocurrencies, providing you with the necessary framework to assess potential investments critically. Later, we'll dive deeper into the unique characteristics of each option.

1. How to spot opportunities

Let's start with the bad news. There is no one way to find the next *cryptocurrency* that will go to the moon (in terms of price action). If that was the case everybody would do it and the law of the market would make it such that nobody would really benefit. On the other hand, the good news is there are some principles for NFTs and Crypto investment you can follow, which you can later personalize.

1.1 Identify your passion

Embarking on an investment journey begins with identifying what resonates with you personally. If you're pondering in which industries you should invest, it's wise to consider areas where your passion and knowledge intersect. Here's why your passion can be your compass to find the right opportunities:

1. **Investing is a marathon, not a sprint.** It requires a sustained commitment, where you'll be expected to regularly monitor your portfolio, make adjustments, and stay informed. Aligning your investments with your passions transforms these tasks from mere responsibilities into enjoyable activities that naturally pique your interest.

2. **Passion breeds insight.** When you invest in industries that you're not just familiar with but genuinely enthusiastic about, you naturally possess a heightened awareness of the sector's nuances. This intimate knowledge grants you the foresight to recognize opportunities that may elude the average investor. You'll also be better able to differentiate between potential breakthroughs and fleeting trends, as you understand the needs and opportunities of your sector.

So, how do you pinpoint the sectors that truly captivate you? **Your current job** is an excellent starting point. The significant chunk of your day spent at work immerses you in the sector's ongoing developments and challenges. It's likely you've experienced firsthand the inefficiencies begging for innovation.

Your leisure activities and hobbies offer inspiration for potential investment opportunities. They might reveal how *Blockchain* or *Web3* could revolutionize activities in which you're already deeply invested in.

Lastly, your **smartphone usage patterns** can offer clues. The type of news you consume, the apps you frequent, and the subjects you gravitate towards – whether it's finance, science, sports, or entertainment – can uncover your investment niches. Don't dismiss these interests as trivial; they could very well lead you to promising ventures within the realms of cryptocurrencies or NFTs.

To find the right projects reflect on moments of frustration or curiosity during your work or leisure activities. Perhaps you had similar thoughts:

- *"If only this solution existed, it would simplify things for me/my clients".*

- *"Why are we still adhering to this outdated method? There's got to be a more efficient way".*

- *"This process doesn't seem fair or transparent. How can we improve honesty and clarity here?"*

These sometimes-fleeting questions often highlight areas ripe for innovation; a clear sign of where you might direct your investment attention. They're not just passing thoughts but compasses which indicate you where you can plant your first investment seeds.

1.2 DYOR (Do your own research)

Embarking on investment decisions with passion is crucial, but it's only one facet of a multi-dimensional process. Passion ignites interest and drives engagement, yet it can sometimes cloud judgment, leading to choices based on emotion rather than facts. This is where the principle of DYOR – Do Your Own Research– becomes invaluable.

DYOR evolved in the *Web3* into a verb that encapsulates the essence of a meticulous and rational approach to investments. It's about peeling back the layers of excitement to scrutinize the core viability and potential of a project.
I will distill DYOR for you to its most fundamental elements, right down to beginner level. DYORing is deep and complex, but by focusing on

the basics, we lay a solid foundation for your investment strategy. As you grow within the crypto space, you'll gradually incorporate more sophisticated elements into your research.

1.2.1 DYOR: The Method

1) Scrutinize the Website & White Paper

A project's website and white paper are its blueprints. A well-crafted website should provide clear information about the team and project goals, while the white paper outlines the project's technology, utility, and vision. Inconsistencies, lack of detail, or poor presentation can be red flags.

2) Check Utility & Use-Case

Any *cryptocurrency* or NFT must have a clear purpose. Does it address a real-world problem or improve an existing process? Consider Bitcoin, it revolutionized financial autonomy by allowing peer-to-peer transactions without banks. This direct response to a genuine need is what fuels its long-standing relevance. Similarly, assess if an NFT brings unique value or artistic merit worthy of its asking price. Research the tokenomics, which means how a token operates within its ecosystem to ensure that there's sustained demand.

3) Do a Team Examination

The people behind the project are the architects of its success. Verify the track record of the developers, advisors, and partners to ensure they have the experience and credibility to deliver on their promises. Be wary of projects that name-drop high-profile individuals without evidence of their involvement.

4) Review the Roadmap

A long-term vision and clear roadmap are indicative of a project's commitment to growth. Look for defined milestones and updates that show progress toward achieving the project's goals. Also check if in the past the project has respected their roadmap. Delivering on time is good indicator for seeing if the project is on track.

5) Engage with Community

The vibrancy of a project's community often mirrors its legitimacy. A strong, knowledgeable base of supporters, developers, and users is an indicator of a project's potential. As mentioned in the previous chapter, platforms like Reddit, Twitter, and Telegram are excellent for gauging community sentiment. Engage with others in forums and on social media to gather diverse perspectives. The collective intelligence of a community can provide insights you might not have considered on your own. A passionate and informed community can signal a project's promising future.

6) Do a Competition Analysis

Consider the project's standing among its competitors. Being the first or best in its category can provide a significant edge. However, new entrants can also disrupt the market with innovative approaches – so weigh the project's merits against existing or upcoming solutions.

7) Look up the Market Cap

Market capitalization offers a snapshot of a project's stability and growth prospects. It's the product of the current price and circulating supply, with higher market caps generally indicating safer investments.

8) Trading Volume & Liquidity

For established cryptocurrencies, trading volume and liquidity are key metrics. They reflect the ease of transactions and can indicate market interest. High trading volume alongside significant price changes can signal market manipulation – so remain vigilant.

9) Circulating vs. Total Supply

Understanding the ratio of circulating to total supply helps gauge potential inflationary impacts. A project with a vast majority of its tokens yet to be released could face dilution, affecting the value of individual tokens.

By diligently applying these facets of DYOR, you'll develop the capacity to discern the wheat from the chaff. It's a lengthy process but your hard-earned money deserves this diligence. The goal is to avoid hopping on every new trend and instead invest in projects with the potential for longevity and meaningful impact. We will now explore how to invest in NFTs and cryptocurrencies. Also, here we will stay on a beginner's level to allow you to make your first investments. As you build your capacities over time, you'll be able to use more complex investments methods.

2. How to invest in NFT

Step 1 - Setting Up Your Crypto Wallet

To kickstart your journey into NFT investing, you'll need a digital wallet, an essential tool for engaging with NFT marketplaces. I already explained how to set up and fund your crypto wallet in Chapter 4. Apply here the steps 2 & 3 mentioned in *"Joining the Web3 wave"*. Most NFT marketplaces are on the Ethereum network, so you'll have to buy Ethereum to buy NFTs. At the end you have to transfer your acquired Ethereum from your Coinbase account to your crypto wallet.

Step 2 - Selecting the Right Marketplace

Your next move is to pick an NFT marketplace that aligns with your interests. Platforms like OpenSea or Rarible are digital bazaars where you can find a diverse array of NFTs. Set up your account on the chosen platform, a process that generally involves providing some personal details and, crucially, linking your crypto wallet to the marketplace.

Step 3 - Connecting Wallet to Exchange

Once you've chosen a marketplace, the actual connection of your crypto wallet should be quite intuitive, especially if you're using a prominent wallet like Metamask. Typically, you'll be prompted to link your wallet through your profile settings on the marketplace. This crucial step allows you to transact, letting you buy, sell, or even create NFTs. Ensure all your information is accurately uploaded, and with that, the world of NFTs is at your fingertips.

Step 4 - Making Your First NFT Purchase

Now comes the exciting part – buying your first NFT! With a funded wallet linked to your marketplace account, you can browse through collections just as you would in any online store. Find an NFT that captures your interest, check the price (be mindful if it's listed in USD or ETH), and when you're ready to make it yours, simply click *"buy"* or place a bid if it's an auction setting – just like any other auction house, you're competing for that unique digital asset.

Now, a quick but crucial word on gas fees: these are the transaction fees on the Ethereum network, and they can be *"painful"*. They're the cost of doing business in the *blockchain* world. Gas fees fluctuate, and sometimes, they can soar so high that they exceed the cost of the NFT itself! If you're new to Ether transactions, keep a keen eye on these fees. They can make or break the deal, and timing your purchase when fees are lower can save you a significant amount. It's all part of the art and strategy of NFT investing. When gas fees are right, confirm your purchase and soon after you'll see your new digital asset in your wallet.

3. How to benefit from Crypto investments

We already explored the *"how"* of buying crypto in Chapter 4 during step 3 and 4 of the subsection *"Joining the Web3 Wave"*. Now, let's delve deeper, and explore the diversity of cryptocurrencies in order to empower your investment choices. We will also discuss practical steps for post-purchase actions, equipping you with the knowledge to maximize your profits in your crypto journey.

3.1 Types of Cryptocurrencies

'Altcoin' stands for 'alternative coin,' a term that captures every digital currency besides Bitcoin (BTC) – though some would extend that distinction to exclude Ethereum (ETH) too, given its unique status and widespread use. These altcoins are often born from forks where developers diverge from Bitcoin or Ethereum to create a new path. Whether it's tweaking the consensus mechanism to improve transaction validation or introducing innovative features that Bitcoin or Ethereum don't offer, altcoins are the diverse offspring of their more famous predecessors, each trying to carve out its niche in the crypto ecosystem.

Though diverse, there are several categories under which we can classify the altcoins we encounter.

- **Payment Tokens**

  Payment tokens like Ethereum, Litecoin or Dash are digital currencies created for the exchange of value. They facilitate transactions between parties, acting as modern-day digital cash.

- **Stablecoins**

  These coins, like USDT and USDC, aim to maintain consistent value, making them a more predictable asset in traders' portfolios. The stability of stablecoins is typically achieved by pegging their value to an underlying asset, such as a fiat currency (e.g., US dollars, euros) or a commodity (e.g., gold). This pegging is often facilitated through mechanisms such as collateralization, reserve backing, or algorithmic controls.

There are different types of stablecoins:

- **Fiat-collateralized stablecoins:** these stablecoins are backed by reserves of traditional fiat currencies, typically held in bank accounts. Each stablecoin in circulation is meant to represent a specific amount of the underlying fiat currency.

- **Commodity-collateralized stablecoins:** these stablecoins are backed by reserves of tangible assets, such as gold or other commodities. The value of the stablecoin is linked to the value of the underlying asset.

- **Algorithmic stablecoins:** these stablecoins use algorithms and smart contracts to maintain their stability. They often rely on mechanisms like expanding or contracting the token supply to adjust the stablecoin's value based on market demand.

- **Security Tokens**

  Security tokens are the bridge between traditional finance and the *blockchain* world, representing real-world assets like stocks or real estate on the *blockchain*. These tokens, regulated by entities like the SEC, offer a new avenue for investment, bringing the assurance of the traditional securities market to the innovative crypto space.

- **Utility Tokens**

  Utility tokens are the fuel for the *blockchain* network, providing access to services and functions within their ecosystems. Ether, for instance, facilitates operations on the Ethereum network, paying for transactions and smart contract executions.

- **Meme Coins**

  Meme coins are the playful side of crypto, born from internet culture and often riding waves of hype and speculation. They capture the whimsical and unpredictable nature of the market, sometimes delivering substantial short-term gains.

- **Governance Tokens**

  Governance tokens grant holders a voice within *blockchain* networks, enabling them to influence decisions and participate in the governance of decentralized platforms. These tokens are emblematic of the shift toward decentralized decision-making in the digital age.

3.2 Post-acquisition

Investing in cryptocurrencies doesn't end with acquisition. With your digital wallet now filled, let's explore the foundational actions and options available to you on a beginners' level: HODL, Staking and Lending.

- **HODL**

  The term 'HODL' has become a rallying cry in the crypto community. It's born from a typo in a 2013 Bitcoin forum where a user meant to say *"hold"* during a turbulent market period.

Now, it has become an acronym for *"Hold On for Dear Life"*. The idea behind it is self-explanatory; HODLing refers to the strategy of holding onto your cryptocurrencies, regardless of market fluctuations, with the belief in their long-term potential. It's a passive investment approach grounded in patience and a vision for future growth.

- **Staking**

  Staking is an active participation method in the crypto world, especially within networks that use Proof of Stake (PoS) and its variants. By staking your coins, you're essentially locking them up to support the network's operations, like transaction validation. In return, you receive rewards, similar to interest in a traditional savings account. It's a process that not only helps secure the network but also offers you a chance to increase your holdings without buying more tokens.

- **Lending**

  Lending in DeFi opens doors to earning interest by loaning out your cryptocurrencies. Through lending protocols, your digital assets can be borrowed by others who often use them for trading or other yield-generating activities. The beauty of this system is the security it offers to lenders. Borrowers must over-collateralize their loans (depositing assets worth more than they borrow) to mitigate the risk to lenders. Should they fail to repay, their collateral ensures you're not left at a loss.

As mentioned before, these three options are only a small portion of what you can do with your crypto investments. Each option has its merits and risks, and it's crucial to align them with your investment goals and risk tolerance. As you gain experience, the complex and vibrant world of DeFi will unveil even more complex strategies like providing liquidity, for maximizing your digital assets.

3.3 Strategizing Your Crypto Portfolio

Crafting your *cryptocurrency* strategy is a personal journey which depends on the intersection of various factors which we defined in this book. If for example your risk tolerance is on the lower end, it could be wise to lean towards stablecoins like USDC or time-tested cryptocurrencies such as Bitcoin and Ethereum, who set the trend for the broader market. For those seeking a more hands-off approach, accumulating these more established coins and holding for long-term appreciation, complemented by staking to earn interest, might suit their style. Alternatively, if you're inclined towards active engagement, governance tokens in emerging projects offer a chance to influence their direction. Active investors might also explore altcoins with solid potential or those offering lucrative lending yield. Ultimately, as these examples show, the right balance will align with your comfort with risk, desired level of involvement, and long-term financial goals.

What to remember

- **Identifying Investment Opportunities:** understand that finding lucrative investments in cryptocurrencies and NFTs requires a blend of passion, knowledge, and diligent research. There's no guaranteed path to success, but certain strategies can guide you.

- **Passion as a Guide:** align your investments with areas you are passionate about. This not only makes the investment journey more enjoyable but also leverages your inherent knowledge and interest in the sector.

- **DYOR (Do Your Own Research):** critical in making informed investment decisions. Examine project websites, white papers, utility, team credibility, roadmaps, community engagement, competition, market cap, and supply metrics.

- **Investing in NFTs:** steps include setting up a crypto wallet, selecting a suitable marketplace, connecting your wallet, and understanding the purchasing process, including considerations like gas fees.

- **Types of Cryptocurrencies:** familiarize yourself with various categories like Payment Tokens, Stablecoins, Security Tokens, Utility Tokens, Meme Coins, and Governance Tokens.

- **Post-Acquisition Strategies:** explore different approaches like HODLing (holding for long-term growth), staking (earning rewards for supporting a network), and lending (earning interest by loaning out cryptocurrencies).

- **Strategizing Your Crypto Portfolio:** tailor your investment strategy based on your risk tolerance, level of engagement, and long-term goals. Consider diversifying across different types of cryptocurrencies and investment methods.

CHAPTER 7

From idea to action: launching your own *Web3* business

"

The world's
biggest problems
are the world's
biggest business
opportunities.

Peter Diamandis

There are ways to engage with *Web3* which go beyond the mere act of financial investment. In this more profound journey, you also become an architect of its future. This path demands more than monetary stakes; it requires your time, dedication, and the very essence of your passion. If you have not guessed it by now, the venture I speak of is none other than entrepreneurship itself.

I would be lying to you if I said that a universal blueprint for business success existed. If things were that simple, everyone would be an entrepreneur, and every endeavor would flourish. I must be honest in saying that starting a business is NOT for everyone. I really believe that being a founder requires having a unique blend of skills, a willingness to embrace uncertainty, and an acceptance of failure.

I think often people associate the entrepreneur's journey with prestige, fame, money, and that can be true sometimes, but they only see the tip of the iceberg. They often overlook the personal and professional sacrifices required. They don't see the patience and the intense dedication before any hint of success, which is always slow to come. I'm not saying this to discourage you, but I want people to be aware of what the journey really represents before they embark on it. Consider for instance these statistics:

- A report by the Small Business Administration (SBA) reveals that about 20% of small businesses fail within the first year, 30% within the second, and 50% by the fifth.[26]

- A Harvard Business School study notes that approximately 75% of venture-backed startups don't succeed.[27]

As you can see, the harsh truth is that startup failures are not the exception but rather a prevalent outcome. Before you begin, brace for potential failure and embrace it as an entrepreneur's rite of

26 Bureau of Labor Statistics. 'Survival of Private Sector Establishments by Opening Year'- https://www.bls.gov/bdm/us_age_naics_00_table7.txt
27 Ghosh, S. (2012, September 19). 'The Venture Capital Secret: 3 out of 4 Start-Ups Fail - News - Harvard Business School' - https://www.hbs.edu/news/Pages/item.aspx?num=487

passage. Many founders face failure multiple times before achieving success. The key is in the perception; seeing not failures, but learning opportunities that pave the way for growth.

This chapter is for those who, after my words of caution, are still interested in this pathless journey. While I can't lay out a foolproof step by step guide, I can offer the wisdom of experience and highlight the critical elements that often determine the fate of *Web3* startups.

1. My entrepreneurial journey

Embarking on the entrepreneurial journey of Utrust (now known as xMoney), I found myself stepping closer to the original team while still at PayPal, where I served as the head of marketplaces divison. My PayPal team's mandate was to craft payment solutions tailored for marketplace platforms. Despite PayPal's mission statement about fostering financial inclusion, I soon faced the harsh reality of opacity, especially regarding customer costs. The lack of clarity and the exorbitant fees associated with international cross-border payments presented a stumbling block, often hindering my team's ability to market the payment platform effectively.

My personal justice compass, which had guided me throughout life, questioned the ethics of our opaque pricing. Why should customers be left in the dark about their financial commitments? Why were international transactions not only prohibitively costly but also a logistical nightmare?

Despite my proposals to PayPal, suggesting we harness *blockchain* to alleviate these issues, my ideas were met with laughter and dismissal, it was 2018, and the concept was too avant-garde for them, (ironically their US division later implemented *blockchain* technology).

Nevertheless, I persisted with my research, and it was during this period of intense study that I stumbled upon a white paper by the original founder of Utrust. The document proposed radical decentralization of banking and credit card systems, aiming to engineer a superior payment framework. Intrigued, I reached out to him on LinkedIn, which quickly led to many passionate online discussions about the future of payment solutions and eventually, face-to-face. After our first in person meeting, it was clear that I wanted to get more involved.

Initially, I functioned as an advisor, scrutinizing the company's direction and prospects for growth. The more I learned, the more invested I became in the vision, culminating in my decision to leave the corporate world behind. This transition wasn't without sacrifice, a cut in salary and a departure from the security provided by the familiar corporate ladder were the prices I had to pay to pursue this novel idea.

After formally joining as a co-founder, I later became CEO. Steering a company which was pioneering in an almost uncharted domain was challenging. Unlike traditional startups where historical precedents offer guidance, we were in untested waters without a compass. It necessitated many radical restructurings: redefining team roles, altering company culture, embracing remote work, and clarifying our vision.

We worked in the beginning under the assumption that the market would eagerly adopt our product, a payment gateway that facilitated crypto to fiat transactions, effectively a PayPal for cryptocurrencies. We launched with the belief that the benefits of cost reduction, elimination of chargebacks, fraud prevention, and access to a new class of assets would be self-evident. However, the reality was quite the opposite; we were addressing a need that was not yet recognized, confined to niche applications, and largely misunderstood.

The challenge, then, was to recalibrate our strategy: not to sell the concept of *blockchain*, but to understand and cater to the immediate needs of our current users. The initial years were tough; client numbers and transaction volumes were low. It necessitated constant pivots, feature launches and deep dives into niche markets where our service could genuinely add value.

From those precarious beginnings, where we questioned the very viability of the company, we've emerged with a clientele of thousands of customers, handling volumes in the millions each month. The path was never clear, and there were moments of profound doubt, but the resilience to pivot from uncertainty to finding a market fit has been an amazing experience.

2. Launching your *Web3* company

As my story shows, there is no one-size-fits-all solution to creating a successful *Web3* company. But I will share with you some principles and points you need to pay attention to in the early stages of your company. There are many more points that will need your attention, but I will focus on those that I would have been happy to hear about at the beginning of my entrepreneurial journey.

2.1 Understand *Web3*

Congratulations on taking a significant step in this field by engaging with this book. But you've only begun to scratch the surface of the expansive world of *Web3*. If you're considering the creation of a *Web3* enterprise, it's crucial to immerse yourself further in its foundational principles, including decentralization, trustless environments, and resistance to censorship. You should start building a deep knowledge of pillars of *Web3* like *Blockchain*s, NFTs, Cryptocurrencies, Smart Contracts, and Oracles.

However, it's essential to beware of becoming an eternal student, which means accumulating knowledge endlessly without ever putting it into practice. A practical assessment of your understanding would be testing your comfort with the terminology and concepts of *Web3*. Attend a conference, summit, or webinar, and when the jargon no longer sounds alien, and you can contribute meaningfully to discussions, you're likely knowledgeable enough to begin.

It's acceptable not to know every facet of *Web3*. With innovations emerging continuously, it's a domain in constant flux, making complete mastery unattainable.

2.2 Assembling Your Dream Team

One main reason startups usually fail is due to a poor fit between founders or disagreements among them. Actually, you would be surprised by how many times this happens!

The reasons behind founder incompatibility can vary, and may include factors such as lack of experience, diverging levels of commitment, disagreements on processes, inability to adapt to changing circumstances, etc.

For this reason, be very aware when choosing who your cofounder/s are going to be. When selecting co-founders, prioritize those you consider trustworthy. Are these people you can easily talk to? Are they self-critical and self-aware enough so that when things are not so great, they have the humility to receive feedback (same question applies to you)? Do you share the same vision? Do you have the same degree of commitment?

Another important characteristic to look for in founders is their ability to have a growth mindset and to continuously learn. You will be challenged many times, and you will have to iterate and adapt. This requires the ability to pivot, learn, and move on.

Relationships of trust are very important, but in the end, you also simply need to be able to get the job done. That is why, in parallel, you have to assess their skills. The more complementary you are, the better, so you can support each other on different topics. Conduct background research and check past achievements, (past or) current positions they hold, or, in the best-case scenario, contributions they've made to other *Web3* projects.

To find the right teammates, first outline the ideal profiles you need, be it in technology, marketing, or other areas. Then, dive into communities and platforms where these individuals gather. *Web3*, with its online-centric culture, offers a borderless recruitment pool. Potential partners and team members, well-versed in *Web3*'s possibilities, are not confined to any single location; they are scattered across the globe. In my experience, I've witnessed many *Web3* entrepreneurs discover their co-founders in virtual spaces like Discord servers.

Alternatively, especially in a later stage, you can also visit *Web3* talent sourcing platforms. They allow you to engage with freelancers on a project basis, assessing their work and dedication before extending an invitation to join your mission. Good examples are CryptoJobsList, and Remote3.co.

2.2.1 Remote Team Management

Remote work is an inherent characteristic in the *Web3* world. For a remote startup, defining the company's structure, rhythm, and roles is important. Begin by creating a digital *"office"*, a virtual space where your team can collaborate. I advocate for Slack workspaces due to their versatility and integration capabilities.

Once your digital domain is established, utilize tools like Trello to delineate roles, responsibilities, and ownership. This setup allows for weekly mission-setting and progress tracking, fostering a performance-oriented culture.

The final piece of the remote work puzzle is establishing a workflow rhythm of regular meetings, calls, and progress reports. These scheduled interactions ensure that despite physical distances, your team remains unified in purpose and direction.

2.2.2 Crafting a Shared Vision

A unified vision is the soul of any team. This vision should not merely be a marketing strategy but the very essence of your team's ethos. A collective genuine *"why"* creates team cohesion and naturally becomes a customer magnet. Referencing Simon Sinek's philosophy, *"People don't buy what you do; they buy why you do it"*.[28] Successful businesses resonate with their audience through a shared set of beliefs and values, cultivating an emotional bond. This alignment not only drives purchases but also fosters loyalty and advocacy. Communicate your *"why"* compellingly, let it echo through every aspect of your startup, from product development to customer service.

In my own journey, the *"why"* was clear: to counteract the inefficiencies in traditional payment systems and to champion financial inclusion. Choose as a team a mission that resonates deeply with you collectively, going beyond monetary motivations. After all, startups founded solely on financial gain rarely reach heights of success. Your *"why"* should be a problem you're passionate about solving, a crusade that resonates with your values and ambitions.

Launching a startup is a time-intensive venture. To prevent burnout and sustain momentum, align your efforts with your passions. Let your startup be more than a collection of jobs; let it be a journey towards contributing to something greater than oneself.

---

28 Sinek, Simon. 2011. 'Start with Why'. Harlow, England: Penguin Books.

2.3 Achieve Product - market fit

A prevalent pitfall for startups, as noted by CB Insights, is launching a product or service without sufficient market demand, a scenario contributing to the downfall of roughly 42% of startups.[29] Founders often become enamored with their vision, bypassing the critical step of market validation. This obsession with one's product or service can lead to a painful realization: the market doesn't share the same affection, resulting in a misalignment between the product and market needs.

To avoid this scenario, engage in customer discovery at the outset. Identify the specific issues your product addresses and the audience dealing with these challenges. This isn't about having a solution in search of a problem; it's about ensuring that there's a clear problem that your solution is uniquely poised to solve.

Then develop an MVP (minimum viable product) based on feedback loops. Pinpoint the essential features that directly solve your customers' pain points and deliver these efficiently. The MVP serves as a beacon, guiding you through the fog of development with user feedback as your compass. The dialogue between your startup and the market will refine each iteration of your product.

As your MVP keeps developing, foster a deeper understanding of your target users. Creating detailed personas and truly understanding the nuances of their pain points allows you to craft tailored solutions that resonate with their needs. These are insights form the backbone of your value proposition, which must be communicated clearly to your prospective users.

This approach helps to build a product that not only meets demand but also anticipates and evolves with the market's shifting dynamics.

---

29 CB Insights. (2022, December 1). 'The top 12 reasons Startups fail'. CB Insights Research. https://www.cbinsights.com/research/report/startup-failure-reasons-top/

2.4 Community and marketing

In the *Web3* ecosystem, your community is not just an audience; they're co-creators, vital in ensuring your product resonates with the market. Their early testing and feedback can be pivotal in achieving product-market fit. A deeply engaged community can even contribute to your project's development, with some members potentially transitioning into key roles within your team, especially when operating remotely. Cultivating your community organically should be a foundational strategy.

Launching your *Web3* project often begins with announcements within community platforms. Initiating conversations on Discord or other major platforms can spark interest. From there, co-creation becomes the driving force. In our experience, we launched with an ICO, drawing an initial community of investors and raising substantial funds. This community lived in our Telegram channels, actively participating in shaping the project's journey, voting on new clients, and contributing to the product's evolution.

This participatory roadmap makes each member feel integral to the product's success. In our case, the most involved community members transitioned into admins and part-time team members, further blurring the lines between users and creators.

However, managing a community comes with its challenges. Commitments to product launches or roadmap milestones that change can stir emotions and dissatisfaction. The antidote is transparency and regular engagement. Treat your community like co-founders by keeping them informed and involved. For instance, we organized monthly Q&As to maintain trust even when our roadmap took unexpected turns.

Cultivating your community organically should be a foundational strategy; paid marketing can come later. A small but active community is more valuable than a large, passive one. It's the quality of interaction that fosters commitment. Once your community is consolidated you can start thinking about paid marketing campaigns. While *Web3* projects once faced advertising challenges on traditional platforms due to regulatory uncertainties, the landscape has evolved. Now, with more clear rules, you can amplify your message across platforms, provided you adhere to their guidelines. Remember, though, that such strategies should only supplement, not replace, the organic community you've nurtured from the beginning.

2.5 Funding your *Web3* startup

When embarking on a *Web3* startup, securing adequate funding is as crucial as the innovation itself. In *Web3*, you have several options to consider. Utilizing personal savings or income from other ventures to fuel your startup's early stages, also called Bootstrapping, is for many founders the foundational approach. This self-funding strategy gives you full control but requires a cautious balance: not hampering growth due to limited financial input but not ruining yourself in the process.

The *Web3* space gave birth to new fundraising methods such as Initial Coin Offerings (ICOs), Security Token Offerings (STOs), and Initial Exchange Offerings (IEOs). These mechanisms, involving the sale of digital tokens associated with your project, can open floodgates of capital. However, the complexity of executing a successful token sale and navigating the labyrinth of regulatory compliance should not be underestimated.

Venture capital and angel investment represent another avenue, offering not just funding but also mentorship and industry contacts.

While this route dilutes some of your autonomy, it's a trade-off for potentially accelerated growth and strategic guidance from seasoned investors who understand the nuances of the *Web3* space.

Once funding is secured, attention must pivot to financial sustainability, primarily cash flow management – a domain where many startups meet their demise. An alarming 82% of startups face failure due to inadequate cash flow.[30] To sidestep this pitfall, you have to develop a detailed financial plan. This plan should meticulously outline your projected expenses, revenue streams, and cash flow forecasts.

Bringing an experienced CFO on board from the get-go can be a game-changer. This person becomes the guardian of your financial stability, continuously monitoring and managing cash flow. I would advise to organize regular financial review sessions with all co-founders to ensure that everyone is informed about the fiscal health of the enterprise.

In summary, funding your *Web3* startup and managing cash flow are two sides of the same coin. Whether through self-funding, innovative token sales, or external investors, securing capital is just the beginning. The real challenge lies in managing that capital wisely to foster a thriving, sustainable business.

Inspiring examples

There are many projects and companies that, in the past few years, have achieved great success in the *Web3* space, as they have either identified better ways to manage old Web2 legacy systems, or they have completely reimagined new ways to do things.

In my years in crypto I had the privilege to see many interesting

---

30 Berry, T. (2007, November 30). '10 critical cash flow rules'. Entrepreneur. https://www.entrepreneur.com/starting-a-business/10-critical-cash-flow-rules/187366

projects, also *"smaller ones"* but that are really challenging the status quo. Here are some projects that inspired me or that I had the pleasure of working with or sit in their advisory boards.

Circle

I love Circle as I really believe stablecoins will be the main means to mass adoption of crypto payments.

Circle's stablecoin, USDC, is a fiat dollar collateralized stablecoin, designed to have a stable value by being pegged to the US dollar. As an ERC-20 token initially built on the Ethereum *blockchain*, USDC has expanded its reach for interoperability by being available on multiple *blockchains*. This strategic move enhances its utility across various ecosystems, all while remaining fully backed by reserves of US dollars held in audited bank accounts.

Circle's USDC stablecoin provides users with a digital representation of US dollars that can be easily transferred, stored, and utilized on various platforms and applications that support it. It aims to bridge the gap between traditional financial systems and the world of cryptocurrencies by providing a stable and transparent digital currency.

Circle has positioned itself as a trusted provider in the crypto space, focusing on regulatory compliance, transparency, and the usability of cryptocurrencies in everyday transactions. It aims to facilitate the mainstream adoption of digital currencies by providing reliable and user-friendly tools and services, and this is why I firmly believe they will be the most used stablecoin globally very soon.
We cannot have mass adoption without collaboration with regulators, traditional institutions and governments, and this is exactly what Circle has been doing for years.

One of my passions and the reason I work in this industry, is the fact that cryptocurrencies, and especially stablecoins, can fuel financial inclusion and really have a huge impact on various applications in humanitarian actions and aid efforts. Here are some potential use cases:

- **Financial Inclusion:** stablecoins can help provide financial access to individuals in regions with limited banking infrastructure. By utilizing digital wallets and USDC, individuals can store and transact with value, even without traditional banking services.

- **Cross-Border Payments:** USDC can be used to facilitate fast and low-cost cross-border payments, enabling efficient transfer of funds to regions affected by crises or in need of humanitarian support. This can help bypass traditional financial intermediaries and reduce transaction costs.

- **Remittances:** stablecoins like USDC can serve as a means for individuals to send remittances to family members or support organizations in regions affected by humanitarian crises. By leveraging *blockchain* technology, remittances can be processed more quickly and securely, potentially reaching recipients in a timelier manner.

- **Transparent Donations:** using USDC as a donation mechanism can provide increased transparency and accountability. Donors can track the flow of funds on the *blockchain*, ensuring their contributions are directed towards the intended beneficiaries and used efficiently.

- **Aid Distribution:** *blockchain*-based systems can be used to track the distribution of humanitarian aid and ensure it reaches its intended recipients. USDC can be utilized to provide digital vouchers or tokens that can be redeemed for essential goods or services in a transparent and accountable manner.

AthenaDAO

AthenaDAO captivates my passion for its mission to revolutionize women's health. Emerging within the Decentralized Science (DeSci), the DAO's ambitious mission is to become a perpetual engine for research that not only funds but also incubates projects focused on women's health, with an emphasis on those areas that, despite their potential to change lives, remain underfunded. AthenaDAO has taken notable strides in this direction, having already financed its inaugural research project into ovarian aging – a field ripe for innovation yet starving for capital.

With AthenaDAO's unique approach to intellectual property (IP), it streamlines the process of funding research, ensuring transparency and efficiency. By leveraging the Molecule's IP-NFT Framework, it acquires and invests in research IP, facilitating IP rights to be issued and traded on the Ethereum *blockchain*. This ensures Athena DAO's ownership or exclusive licensing rights which represents a groundbreaking innovation in scientific funding.

Governance within AthenaDAO is exercised through the $ATH token, enabling holders to vote on key decisions such as research investments, commercialization strategies, and DAO operations. This process empowers token holders to actively participate in the DAO's direction, fostering a democratic and community-centric model of operation.

As a passionate advocate for AthenaDAO, I am inspired by its dedication to funding critically underfunded yet vitally important research, specifically on conditions like PCOS and Endometriosis. By championing translational and transformative research, AthenaDAO is in the pole position to make tangible improvements in health for women around the world. The project's success in raising funds and backing significant research is a testament to the power of collective action and innovative funding models. As Athena DAO continues to grow, I'm looking forward to see its plans to broaden its research scope and amplify awareness of women's health issues become a reality.

What to remember

- **Embrace the Entrepreneurial Spirit:** entrepreneurship in Web3 is a commitment to innovation and shaping the future, requiring time, dedication, and passion.

- **Accept the Reality of Failure:** be aware that failure is a common outcome in startups. It's important to view failures as learning opportunities that contribute to growth rather than as defeats.

- **Know Your 'Why':** your startup should be driven by a collective mission that resonates with you deeply. Communicate your vision compellingly to create an authentic connection with your audience.

- **Deep Understanding of Web3:** immerse yourself in the principles of Web3, including decentralization and trustless environments, but avoid the trap of becoming an eternal student without practical application.

- **Building Your Team:** choose co-founders and team members who are not only skilled and trustworthy but also share your vision and commitment. Embrace remote work and leverage digital tools for collaboration.

- **Market Fit Is Key:** start with customer discovery to ensure your product solves a real problem. Use the feedback to refine your MVP and align it closely with market needs.

- **Community Engagement:** your community is a co-creator in your Web3 project. Engage with them transparently and leverage their feedback to achieve product-market fit.

- **Financial Planning and Funding:** consider various funding options, including bootstrapping, ICOs, STOs, and IEOs. Prioritize financial sustainability by managing cash flow effectively, and consider hiring an experienced CFO early on.

CHAPTER 8

Building a culture of inclusion: overcoming the Bro culture

"

*Turn your wounds
into wisdom.*

Oprah Winfrey

Embarking on a journey into the Crypto and *Web3* worlds, you'll notice something striking – the scarcity of women. As you attend conferences and engage with online communities, it becomes clear that despite *blockchain*'s potential for women empowerment, it largely remains a boys' club. The numbers tell a stark tale: merely 13% of *Web3* startups include a woman on their founding team, and only 3% are all-women. In the wider *Web3* workforce, women make up just over a quarter, often filling non-technical roles.[31] In the NFT world, women represent only 16% of artists and a mere 5% of sales. As for crypto investing, just 26% are women[32].

In this chapter, we'll tackle the prevailing *"bro culture"* in the crypto space, examining where it comes from and the effect it has. We'll discuss how we can challenge this status quo as a community, and I'll share some practical advice with you for navigating through it. And to inspire, I'll highlight some incredible women who are making waves in *Web3*.

1. The Bro culture

So, what is the bro culture about? The *"bro culture"* in *Web3* isn't only about who's coding or leading; it's about a certain vibe that fills the room. It's like a private club where jokes, competition, and an easy camaraderie set the tone, and it often leans on a mix of ego, lingo and mutual support among men. This culture can be friendly and informal, sure, but it also excludes many women who might feel themselves on the outside looking in.

31 Apotheker, J., Hazan, J., Marteau, P., Cho, P., Srinivasan, S., Berry, S., & Hamid, A. (2023, February 16). 'Web3 already has a gender diversity problem'. BCG Global. https://www.bcg.com/publications/2023/how-to-unravel-lack-of-gender-diversity-web3#:~:text=BCG%20X%2C%20the%20tech%20and,team%20that%20is%20exclusively%20female.
32 Zavo, L. (2022, January 28). 'Can women turn the tables and diversify the NFT art space?' Forbes. https://www.forbes.com/sites/forbesbusinesscouncil/2022/01/28/can-women-turn-the-tables-and-diversify-the-nft-art-space/?sh=1716931668bb

1.1 Origins

How can an industry that promotes decentralization and equal opportunities for everyone get into this situation? Why has this culture taken such a firm hold in *Web3*? By breaking it down we realize that there are 3 main reasons:

1. **Historical Imbalance:** from the start, crypto and *blockchain* were in the beginning mainly side projects for tech enthusiasts and developers – primarily men. This isn't new; tech has long been a male stronghold. Just peek inside any major tech company; you'll see the higher you go, the fewer women you find. With only about 20%[33] of developers in the U.S. being women and even fewer in the boardrooms, it's clear this imbalance didn't just disappear when *Web3* came along.

2. **Lack of Representation:** it's a cycle that feeds itself; fewer women in tech means fewer women finding their way into *blockchain*. Without female voices in key roles, the direction and decisions lean male. Without women to look up to, many can't even picture themselves in this world, making it hard to break the cycle and thus leaving the industry to men.

3. **Gender Bias:** then there's the subtler side; biases that can make the playing field uneven. Take funding: teams with just men often get nearly four times the funding of all-women teams. Much of the investment world is men investing in other men. It's based on the cognitive bias that we like to invest in people that we can relate to, hence that look like us. Unfortunately, this bias unintentionally edges women out of opportunities and further increases the lack of representation.

---

33 *'Stack Overflow Developer Survey 2020'. (n.d.). Stack Overflow. https://insights.stackoverflow.com/survey/2020*

One could say the *Web3* larger community snowballed itself into this situation. Luckily this means even if deeply rooted the bro culture is not an inherent characteristic of *Web3*. It's a vestige it took over from its origins and that has for a long time not been addressed. This negligence of the situation has had negative impacts not only for women but for the *Web3* space as a whole.

1.2 Impact of the Bro culture

As most things the Bro culture has its good points, but it also comes with many negative consequences which hinder *Web3* to realize its full potential:

Marginalizing Women and Others

As mentioned before, the Bro culture in *Web3* creates an unwelcoming environment for anyone who doesn't fit the crowd. And I want to be clear here, this does not only concern women but also men who do not adhere to these norms. They, too, can feel alienated in these bro-dominated settings, choosing to leave or avoid the *Web3* world altogether.

Creating Toxic Work Environments

When the bro culture runs unchecked in companies, it can evolve into a hyper-masculine and overly competitive workspace, toxic to anyone who isn't part of the *"in"* crowd. This doesn't just lead to discomfort; it can create a work environment filled with stress and mental health issues, making it unsustainable for those who want to contribute their ideas and talents freely and safely.

Hindering Innovation

A mono-cultural approach to *Web3* blocks innovation by limiting the range of perspectives that contribute to problem solving. When women and other diverse groups are pushed out, it's not just their presence that's lost, it's also their ideas, insights, and unique perspectives. This loss narrows the scope of creativity and can cause the industry to miss out on innovative breakthroughs that could transform the sector.

Turning Potential Investors Away

The brashness of the extreme *"crypto bros"* can repel those who might otherwise be interested in the field. Their hyperfocus on potential high profits and a show-off lifestyle can be off-putting, deterring a broader range of investors. For *Web3* to achieve its potential and attract the next billion users, embracing inclusivity and welcoming women is mandatory.

Unstable Markets

Research into gender differences in risk-taking reveals that women typically exhibit more caution when it comes to investing, which could lead to more stable markets. Men's optimism often translates into a greater willingness to take risks. If a high number of people participate in very risky investments, this can result in very volatile markets. More gender-balanced participation in the crypto markets could result in a healthier, less volatile investing environment, benefiting the industry as a whole.

This shows clearly that the bro culture's negative consequences outweigh its potential positive aspects. As the vision of *Web3* was never to be a man-only club, we have to gradually transition to creating a more inclusive industry. *Web3* has the unique opportunity to show the industry tech as a whole how it's done instead of settling with the status quo. So, what can we do to forge an inclusive space that encourages women to join and thrive? What areas need our attention?

2. Countering the male dominance

Here are some strategies which I believe could bring systemic change and alter the existing dynamics. Let's be honest, it's a complex topic but I'm convinced that this multifaceted approach could be a game changer.

Education and Awareness

Education is the cornerstone of change. Raising awareness about the gender imbalance is the first step toward creating an inclusive *Web3* environment. By spotlighting the importance of diversity and educating communities, we can break down stereotypes and encourage more women to explore opportunities in *blockchain* and *Web3*. Educational initiatives need to also reach out to young women, offering them the resources and knowledge to envision a future in *Web3*.

Promoting Female Role Models

Visibility of women's achievements in *Web3* is crucial for inspiring the next generation. We need to amplify the successes of women in the space, ensuring they have prominent roles at conferences and are featured in dedicated *Web3* news outlets. By promoting female role models actively and consciously, we not only celebrate their accomplishments but also demonstrate to women everywhere that they have a significant place in this industry.

Inclusive Communities

We have to keep toxicity out of our *Web3* communities by installing zero-tolerance policies towards discrimination and harassment. We have to foster supportive cultures where inclusivity is the norm. This will help women to contribute their ideas and talents freely, without the fear of marginalization.

Creating Spaces for Women

Dedicated spaces where women can connect, share insights, and support each other are vital. These can take the form of online forums, local meetups, or international conferences. By providing arenas where women can collaborate and lead, we create opportunities for them to influence the direction of *Web3*.

Diverse Leadership

Balanced leadership is key to driving forward the principles of equality within *Web3*. Encouraging women to assume leadership roles ensures diverse perspectives at the decision-making table. For a limited time, one could envision the introduction of quotas until an even playing ground is established.

A good doctor does not stop at the symptoms of a patient but tries to understand the root causes of the disease. In the same way I believe the bro culture is not the main problem but simply the manifestation of a lack of female presence in *Web3*. That is why we should focus our energy on creating the right conditions for women to enter the *Blockchain* space. By implementing these initiatives, each of us can contribute to dismantling gradually the male dominance.

3. Navigating the Bro culture

The bro culture in the *Web3* space is currently an undeniable reality and while waiting for cultural shift, women have to learn navigating it. Let's explore how to find our way while also enjoying the process.

Join the Ride While Staying Authentic

Given the circumstances, we have to make the best out of the situation. This means for me participating in the space and enjoying the ride. I am a strong believer in bringing change from within. For example, as a female CEO in *Web3*, I have found that learning the lingo and signing deals in the (very) early hours are integral aspects of this space. Deals often come together based on casual conversations at a bar around a beer rather than formal proposals. This happened to me on a weekly basis. This sounds like fun, and it actually is but I also asked myself on multiple occasions: *"What am I doing here?"* These episodes highlight again the importance of having a strong *"why"*, but you should also be very clear about your values. Define for yourself how far you are willing to go and what are red flags that indicate that you are not being true to yourself anymore. Don't shy away from speaking up when you feel something is not right. Always remember that, no matter the situation you find yourself in, you are in power. You have the power of how you feel. So, if you're giving someone else – and that usually is a man – the power to make you feel in a particular way, that is your decision. In the end you are in charge. Use your hidden superpower to say no. Say *"no"* to things…

- that make you feel uncomfortable,

- diminish your worth,

- contradict your values,

- force inauthenticity upon you.

If the idea of joining the *"boys club"* doesn't resonate with you, consider forging one-on-one connections. This approach can transform people into allies. For instance, while I was CEO at Utrust, we corresponded via email with a prospective real estate client from Turkey. The CEO had assumed I was male, misled by my name which, in Indian culture, is typically male. Imagine his astonishment during our first video call when he discovered his counterpart was a woman! After the initial surprise, which was a mix of confusion and revelation, the dynamic shifted positively. He'd rarely encountered women in leadership roles within *Web3*, and it was a refreshing change for him. That interaction marked the beginning of a beautiful alliance; he became not just a client, but my biggest supporter, advocating for my role and contributions wherever he could.

Take a personal inventory

As mentioned previously, to navigate this culture, knowing yourself is key. Assess your career, passions, and what balance means to you. Maintain regular self-checks. Are your actions in line with your aspirations? Do they resonate with your inner sense of balance? It's essential to establish these parameters to remain true to yourself amidst external pressures.

In my own journey, mindfulness and spiritual practices have been anchors in stormy moments. These regular exercises and retreats are reminders of who I am at my core, guiding my decisions to be in harmony with my true self. They've allowed me to stand firm in my values, make choices that reflect my authenticity, and navigate the industry with integrity.

Find a community

Remember you are not alone. There are countless women, from those just starting to industry veterans, who share similar challenges. Reaching out to them can provide you a powerful network, offering mutual support. Tapping into a community of *Web3* women that walk the same path as you can significantly propel your personal and professional growth.

Never settle for less

Settling for less is a common trap. Often, women accept initial offers without negotiating. Over time, I learned to ask myself 'What would a man do in this scenario? What would he ask for? Not all aspects of bro culture are bad. Accepting less can sometimes be a sign of humility and contentment, both admirable traits. However, there's absolutely no harm in asserting your worth and requesting what you truly deserve. It's a lesson I've learned from watching men negotiate: they don't shy away from advocating for their value, and neither should you.

Get comfortable with self-advocating

"How Women Rise", a book by Sally Helgesen and Marshall Goldsmith, sheds light on behaviors that often hold women back professionally.[34] One of the key points it discusses is the struggle women face with self-promotion. There's a tendency to downplay achievements, a hesitation to step into the spotlight and own one's accomplishments. But here's the thing: if you don't affirm your own value, how can you expect others to recognize it?

In *Web3* a lot of networking is happening. In this frame as an investor or entrepreneur, your ability to articulate your worth is critical. The goal is not to boast or exaggerate, as we've seen some men may do, but to open doors to potential collaborations by confidently presenting what you bring to the table.

For those of us for whom self-advocating feels like a real agony, it's helpful to reframe the narrative. Early in my career, the idea of public speaking was terrifying. The breakthrough came when I shifted the focus from myself to my audience. Every time I'd step up to speak, I'd center my thoughts on a service attitude. What insights can I offer that will enrich their lives? How can my experiences benefit them? This shift from self-centered apprehension to a service-oriented approach can dissolve fears and self-doubt.

When you speak from a place of service, the personal pressure eases. It's no longer about you or your ego; it's about the value you're providing.

34 Helgesen, S., & Goldsmith, M. (2019). 'How women rise: Break the 12 habits holding you back'. Random House Business Books.

This mindset not only alleviates the discomfort of self-promotion but also, quite beautifully, ends up enhancing your standing. Ultimately, when you share your knowledge and experience generously, people associate that value with you. They remember not only contribution but also the contributor.

Lead with grace

If you are in a leadership role in a *Web3* organization or community, use your attributes to foster inclusive environments. The ethos of *Web3* and crypto is to *"create new models that make the old ones obsolete"*. In the same tenure we should not reinforce the existing Bro culture but set new standards. Going back to *"How Women Rise"*, it suggests that women's leadership often incorporates empathy, inclusivity, and emotional intelligence, traits that are crucial for nurturing a healthy workplace culture. When women lead, they bring a collaborative spirit that can transform company dynamics, encouraging diverse ideas and fostering a sense of belonging. By embracing these traits, we can create leadership styles which impact positively our individual organizations and more importantly set precedents for the industry at large. In this way slowly a new industry culture can emerge, paving the way for more women to join the ride.

What to remember

- **Understanding the landscape and the Bro culture:** the Web3 and Crypto world are currently male-dominated, with women making up a small percentage of the workforce. Bro culture in Web3 is a pervasive attitude that can exclude those who don't fit its norms. This culture has roots in historical imbalances and a lack of representation in tech, leading to a cycle of exclusion. It has far-reaching consequences beyond just a lack of diversity. It can create toxic work environments, hinder innovation, turn away potential investors, and lead to unstable markets. It's essential to understand these impacts to address Bro culture effectively.

- **Education and awareness:** advocate for and contribute to educational initiatives that highlight the importance of diversity and the role of women in shaping the future of Web3.

- **Celebrating female achievements:** we have to amplify the visibility of women in Web3 through active promotion and representation at industry events and in media. This not only honors their

contributions but also sets a precedent for
what women can achieve in the industry.

- **Authentic participation:** engage with
  the Web3 community while maintaining
  personal integrity, setting clear values and
  boundaries.

- **The power of community:** leverage
  the strength of networks of women in
  Web3 for support, guidance, and shared
  experiences to navigate the industry
  together. This community can act as a
  source of encouragement, and a powerful
  alliance in driving change within the Web3
  ecosystem.

- **Asserting worth:** embrace negotiation and
  self-advocacy to affirm the value of your
  contributions. Don't hesitate to voice your
  achievements, and share your insights
  generously. By doing so you pave the way
  for others to assert their worth as well.

- **Leadership with empathy:** lead with
  emotional intelligence and inclusivity,
  utilizing female attributes to create
  a more welcoming and cohesive work
  environment, and inspire industry-wide
  change.

CHAPTER 9

Preparing for the future: cashing out and navigating exit strategies

*Great is the art
of beginning,
but greater is
the art of ending.*

Henry Wadsworth
Longfellow

There comes a moment when it is time to enjoy the rewards of your investments. Having an abundance mindset doesn't only apply to the accumulation of wealth; it's also about acknowledging when to savor the success. This chapter is about precisely that: learning to secure and benefit from the profits you've made, and understanding the steps to gracefully exit the company you've helped to build.

1. Transforming crypto into wealth

Cashing out from *cryptocurrency* investments is a crucial part of the investment lifecycle. To successfully secure profits you have to be familiar with market conditions, particularly the cyclical nature of bull and bear markets, which are terms borrowed from the broader finance world. We need first to understand these cycles through which the crypto market goes as a whole to find the right moments to cash out.

1.1 Bear vs Bull market

In the context of *cryptocurrency*, **a bull market** is characterized by rising prices and optimism. Investors are eager to buy in, driven by the belief that the upward trend will continue, leading to new all-time highs for many of the top 50 cryptocurrencies. It's a phase where the market sentiment is driven by a strong belief in the future of cryptocurrencies. Typically, these periods correlate with key events such as Bitcoin halvings. The Bitcoin halving is a scheduled event that cuts the reward for mining new blocks in half, occurring approximately every four years. This event reduces the rate at which new bitcoins are generated, effectively diminishing supply and, if demand remains strong, potentially driving up the price. This scarcity principle is a fundamental economic driver that often leads to a surge in Bitcoin's value, thereby stimulating a broader bull market.

Conversely, **a bear market** reflects a downturn, where prices fall, sentiment is low, and investors are wary. It can lead to periods known as 'crypto winters,' where prices stagnate or decline over a prolonged period. These phases can be disheartening, with high levels of fear and uncertainty.

1.2 Cash out methods

There exists a wide variety of options that allow you to convert your *cryptocurrency* profits into tangible rewards. Each method of cashing out has its merits and drawbacks, and the best approach depends on your immediate needs and long-term financial goals.
Using the right method ensures that you can capitalize effectively on your digital assets.

Direct Retail Purchases

A direct and increasingly popular method of utilizing crypto earnings is through retail purchases. An expanding number of businesses now accept cryptocurrencies like Bitcoin. Whether it's for a cappuccino at Starbucks, getting accessory from Tesla's catalog or everyday items from a local store, the *"Buy with Bitcoin"* option is becoming commonplace. Retailers typically display a Bitcoin sticker or symbol at checkout to signal their crypto-friendly status.

Money Transfer Apps

Transfer apps have transformed into mini crypto exchanges. Platforms such as PayPal, Revolut and Cashapp now offer integrated services to buy and sell crypto. However, your crypto must have been purchased in the app as these platforms don't allow for the transfer of external crypto holdings for selling. Also, there is a limited selection of cryptocurrencies you can interact with; for instance, Cash App supports only Bitcoin, and PayPal expands to a few others. What they lack in choice, these apps compensate in user-friendliness as they provide a straightforward selling process with reasonable fees.

Crypto ATMs

Around the world, we see that Bitcoin ATMs become commonplace, located in everyday places like gas stations or grocery stores. They offer a physical point where you can purchase and, in some cases, sell your Bitcoin or Altcoins. Selling requires a few steps, including identity verification and sending Bitcoin from your digital wallet to the ATM, which then dispenses cash.

Crypto Debit Cards

For those who prefer the familiarity of a card swipe, crypto debit cards offered by exchanges like Coinbase provide a seamless way to spend crypto. Linked directly to your exchange account, these cards automatically convert your chosen *cryptocurrency* to fiat currency for purchases, and may offer rewards in the form of crypto deposited back into your account. Additionally, these cards can be used at ATMs for cash withdrawals, with certain limits and potentially minimal fees. By now, there are many providers of such crypto debit cards. Compare different offers to make sure you get the best deal for your *cryptocurrency*.

Fiat Exchange via Crypto Exchanges

Centralized crypto exchanges are perhaps the most used method for turning your digital currency into fiat. They offer a broad selection of cryptocurrencies and supported fiat currencies. There is an unwritten rule that applies to most centralized exchanges; simplicity comes at a cost, which means the more straightforward the method is on the exchange to turn your crypto into fiat, the higher the fees will be. Consider this before clicking the *"sell my crypto"* button, and maybe circumvent these fees by opting for the internal Advanced Trade platform, though it presents a more complex interface.

1.3 Strategic Considerations for Cashing Out

In the realm of *cryptocurrency* investment, a tactical approach can make all the difference. Here are some considerations that can help you craft your cash out strategy.

Market timing

It's nearly impossible to perfectly time the market. When it comes to Bitcoin, for example, some self-proclaimed analysts come up with outlandish high price predictions that are based on no fundamentals, and on the other side, very renowned institutions have called it dead at least 1,000 times since I became an investor. However, even if it's very difficult to predict the market, understanding its cycles allows us to adopt the best behavior. The common investment strategy of 'buy low, sell high' is particularly pertinent in the crypto market. During bear markets, when prices dip and sentiment is wary, buying assets at a discount can set you up for potential gains in the next bull market. Conversely, during bull markets that are driven by investor greed, selling is the best option as assets may reach peak overvaluation. Tools like CoinMarketCap's greed barometer help investors to visualize the market sentiment, signaling when the market may be getting overheated.

Stablecoin conversion

To secure profits, consider converting a portion of your *cryptocurrency* to a stablecoin like USDC. This creates a buffer from market fluctuations. However, this move also means stepping away from potential future gains.

Long-term vision

It's essential to weigh immediate gains against future potential. If you believe in the long-term prospects of your assets, consider maintaining your position to benefit from future appreciation. One strategy is to safeguard your principal investment while using DeFi tools like staking or lending to generate yield. This way, you can cash out the yield without diminishing your principal holdings, allowing you to reap the rewards of your investment while still benefiting from positive market swings.

Tax implications

Understanding the tax consequences of selling *cryptocurrency* is crucial. Since crypto is treated as property for tax purposes, selling at a higher price than the purchase price could incur capital gains taxes in many countries. Crypto tax software can help you track transactions and calculate for your tax liability.

Fees

Selling crypto isn't without costs. While many exchanges offer reasonable rates, other avenues like crypto ATMs may impose high fees that erode your profits. Before selling, review the fees, which are typically listed transparently on most platforms. Generally, centralized exchanges or online brokers offer more favorable rates than other services.

2. Exiting your startup

Deciding to leave your startup can arise for a variety of reasons. You might have a new idea that doesn't fit your current business, or perhaps the day-to-day has become too routine. Maybe your interests have shifted towards philanthropy, impact investing, or you're simply craving more time for personal life and family. Exiting isn't a one-size-fits-all process; it can take many forms, like handing over your shares to a partner, orchestrating a management buyout (MBO), or even going public (IPO).

However, in this section, I'll delve into mergers and acquisitions (M&A), a process I'm familiar with from personal experience. I'll share practical insights, aiming to equip you with knowledge I wish I had at the outset. This will allow you to leave your company in a position that's beneficial for you and your team.

2.1 Anticipate your exit

Planning your exit from your startup shouldn't be a thought reserved for the final hour; it's a strategy that begins on day one. It is crucial to define your objectives early on. Understanding what you want to achieve with your startup will help you develop specific exit criteria. For instance, you might set goals such as reaching a particular revenue threshold, obtaining a certain number of users, achieving a key technological breakthrough, or capturing a defined percentage of the market. Consider these benchmarks not as obligations to sell, but as milestones. You and your co-founders can always decide to continue the journey together. These criteria serve as orientation points that offer the autonomy to choose an exit that aligns with your vision rather than succumbing to unforeseen circumstances.

At Utrust, we didn't have such criteria, but we always kept one eye on the future, constantly questioning potential scenarios. Our motto was practical: *"leaders anticipate, losers react"*. This mindset allowed us for instance to anticipate a bear market. Looking at our startup, we realized that it was in a robust state, its growth trajectory was positive, and we were in the middle of a bullish market. We understood that we had no pressing incentive to sell our company, which placed us in a favorable position with all cards on our side. Reflecting on this experience there is one insight crystalizing; the best moment to sell your company is when you don't have to, when you're in the driver's seat, able to set the pace and exit gracefully, without pressure.

2.2 Find the right partners.

To find the right acquisition partner for your startup you have to position yourself within their ecosystem. It's essential to engage actively in business networks, attend industry fairs, and partake in conferences where potential acquirers are present, because when the moment comes that you want to sell, you'll want to have already built up your network of potential buyers.

During our own startup journey at Utrust, we started to subtly communicate our openness to a merger or acquisition within our network as we wanted to anticipate the next market shifts. This led to four companies showing interest. In parallel our participation in a prestigious accelerator program in San Francisco culminated in a demo day, pitching to a host of venture capitalists. This exposure resulted in multiples expressions eagerness to raise funds with us. This interest from different kinds of entities empowered us and shifted the dynamic in our favor, where we went from pitchers to suddenly be the interviewers.

Early on, we realized that aligning with a venture capitalist wasn't our path; we sought a strategic partner with the capacity to elevate our product. Initially, we gravitated towards the largest company that was interested in us. To be honest, we pivoted towards them mainly because of the potential financial gains. However, as negotiations progressed, it became clear that our values did not align. Their approach to undervaluing Utrust and their less-than-ideal treatment of our team highlighted the cultural mismatch. Withdrawing from that deal, despite the sunk time and effort in negotiation and due diligence, was a tough but necessary decision. It is easy to be swayed by the impressive figures that float around during M&A discussions, but in the end, it has to be your foundational principles that guide your decisions. After that experience we regrouped, prioritizing our values over money.

By looking at what united us as co-founders, we wanted to continue our journey with a partner that would resonate with our humble beginnings. This led us to pivot towards a smaller company from Romania, with which we could relate. Multiverse X was founded by two brothers who also had to build everything from scratch. We really enjoyed their humble approach and they shared our entrepreneurial spirit and work ethic. Besides the cultural fit, there was huge potential for our combined growth and the synergy between our products was clear. They were developing a layer one *blockchain* and a decentralized exchange but lacked a payment gateway and ecosystem – components Utrust could provide. This chemistry led to the acquisition by Multiverse X.

Our experience shows that selling your company is a test of resilience and clarity. The process is demanding, mirroring the flexibility and tenacity you already have to develop to make your startup grow. Avoid the pitfalls of greed, and focus on the broader vision. seek a partner that not only aligns with your values, but also propels you toward your goals.

Negotiate & Due diligence

Once a potential buyer shows interest in your startup, it's time to prepare for the crucial stage of negotiation. Your approach should be shaped by **clear objectives**: are you aiming for a complete exit to enjoy retirement, or to fund your next business venture? Perhaps you wish to maintain some involvement? Answering these questions with your co-founders will guide you in setting the ideal and minimum acceptable outcomes for the deal. Entering negotiations from a position of strength is essential. A thriving startup with favorable macroeconomic conditions empowers you to aim high.

During negotiations don't get blinded by money. More important are the clauses linked to it. Make sure that stipulations regarding

compensation and earn-out conditions are crystal clear. Many acquirers expect you to stay on your team for a while (1-5 years) to guarantee a smooth handover, often with compensations linked to your team hitting certain targets. It's vital to ensure that these goals, and the conditions to unlock full compensation, are explicit and non-negotiable later on. In these discussions, never be ashamed to seek clarification on any point; it's better to ask twice than to leave misunderstandings unresolved.

In the *Web3* domain, often compensation gets linked to *cryptocurrency*. For instance, Multiverse X proposed an earn-out partly in their tokens. However, given the volatility of crypto, especially during bear markets, it's wise to minimize the crypto portion of the earnout. The exit should be a time to enjoy the fruits of your labor without worrying about the fluctuating value of your compensation. If crypto is to be part of the payment, stablecoins are the safer choice.

Lastly, don't forget your team. They've been instrumental in your success and should be considered in the terms of the acquisition. Informing them about the process and finding ways for them to benefit from the deal is vital. While equity sharing might set unrealistic expectations, bonuses or other creative rewards, such as vacation, can positively motivate the team during the earnout phase and ensure a successful transition.

Post-negotiation, you'll encounter the most challenging phase: **due diligence**. The intensity of this process varies, but it involves legal teams scrutinizing every aspect of your business; from financial health to security protocols, operational processes, and even employees. It involves a deep dive into the quality of the team, product, and internal processes. The acquiring company needs to affirm the legitimacy of operations and the veracity of financial statements. This phase can be exhaustive, often taking a significant amount of time, spanning six months from the first engagement to completion in our case.

As a founder, especially if you're the CEO, you're central to this process. You'll attend numerous meetings and provide extensive data. Sometimes, this data may not be even available, requiring manual collection – a very time-consuming task. That's why gathering data proactively throughout your company's growth is advantageous. If your end goal is to exit your startup sooner or later, make sure to gather crucial data from the beginning; it will save you a lot of time down the road.

In this phase maintaining close contact with your mentors and peers can provide perspective, reassuring you that the stress and demands are a normal part of the process.

Simply be mindful that due diligence demands a lot of energy and resources that you won't be able to direct toward business development. Moreover, this is all undertaken without any guarantee of a finalized deal, requiring from you a high degree of resilience and detachment from the outcome.

2.3 Transition out

The ink is dry, the deal is done, and what unfolds now is your transition out of the company you've nurtured. Post-deal, the initial wave of relief might soon be met with what a Forbes article describes as post-deal depression (PDD) – an emotional dip following the high stakes of a business sale.[35]

Two primary factors contribute to PDD. The first is the fleeting joy associated with the acquisition's culmination. After the celebration subsides, you're plunged back into the grind to hit targets for your earnout. This dissonance can leave you questioning why the sense of

35 Lehne, L. (2023, June 26). 'How to overcome Post-Deal Depression after an acquisition'. Forbes. https://
www.forbes.com/sites/forbesagencycouncil/2023/06/26/how-to-overcome-post-deal-depression-after-an-
acquisition/?sh=302e0e3313ce

accomplishment isn't as profound as expected. The intensity of the due diligence process is often underestimated, creating unrealistic high expectations of the post-acquisition reality.

The second factor contributing to PDD is a feeling of loss. When you sell your company, it can suddenly feel as though it's no longer part of you. This shift in identity can lead to a profound sense of emptiness, which many founders underestimate. It's a common narrative, one I've seen repeatedly, including within our team at Utrust.

From a preventive point of view, combating PDD starts now for you. If you believe that you'll be happy once you reach your goals, then you are setting yourself up for PDD. Don't wait for lightning to strike to allow yourself to be happy. Learn to enjoy the moment. It might sound cliché, but it's about savoring the journey, appreciating the little day-to-day gifts and maintaining an abundance mindset.

If PDD still sets in, be kind to yourself, treat it with self-compassion. If it kicked in it has a reason. It means you have been chasing a mirage. Embrace the questions that fill your mind. They will guide your introspection and way out of PDD.

In the immediate aftermath of the M&A deal, connecting with peers who've traversed this path can offer support and practical advice. Also make your mental health your priority in your newfound free time. On the other hand, don't become too self-absorbed. Consider extending support to others from your team involved in the M&A, they are probably going through the same experience as you.

In the long term, embrace the fact that selling your business is a transformative period similar to retirement. It's a transition marked by reinvention and self-discovery, and it won't always be easy. Mourning the past while adjusting to the new normal is part of the process, and finding your rhythm again might take time.

Create a game plan for the initial post-exit phase, setting three to five goals to provide structure.

With this framework, you can create a routine that eases the transition. In their white paper *"How Entrepreneurs Transition to the Next Stage"*, Barbara B. Roberts and Murray B. Low explain that finding your way back into your 'flow state' after exiting can take anywhere from one to even six years. Through the cases they interviewed they found that getting back your flow is directly linked to understanding what is your next *"fulfilling chapter"*. This fulfilling chapter is characterized by a feeling of absorption in your new endeavor. Many found themselves in activities such as impact investment, philanthropy, community activities, service projects and teaching. Interestingly, many cases described a phase of 'unfulfilling wandering' before finding the next chapter. During this period, they would do amazing things such as traveling the world, continuing their learning journey, launching new companies, or, like me, publishing a book.[36]

Life has a way of presenting unforeseen opportunities, and sometimes your next fulfilling chapter might just find you. That's exactly what unfolded in my journey. Though my initial plan was to step back, delve into angel investing, and ponder over my next venture, a compelling opportunity with Circle surfaced unexpectedly, and I decided to seize it. Our journeys aren't predestined or fixed; they're shaped by our own insights, decisions and feelings. By staying attuned to our inner compass, we're always prepared to step forward into the next chapter, whenever it may present itself.

This shows that there is no one fit next chapter for everybody, so explore this period of your life with an open heart and embrace your curiosity. What ignites your passion? What brings you joy?

---

36 B. Roberts, B., & B. Low, M. (2013). *'How Entrepreneurs Transition to the Next Stage'. Columbia Business School.*

It may take years to settle into a new rhythm, but the journey there can be filled with growth and self-discovery. This isn't just a pause; it's an opportunity for some of the most significant personal development of your life.

What to remember

- **Cashing Out and Market Conditions:** understand the cyclical nature of cryptocurrency markets to time your cash out effectively. Familiarity with bull and bear market conditions is essential for maximizing returns on your investments.

- **Diverse Withdrawal Methods:** explore various cash out methods for cryptocurrency profits, from direct retail purchases to money transfer apps, crypto ATMs, crypto debit cards, and fiat exchanges via crypto exchanges. Choose the method that aligns with your immediate needs and long-term financial goals.

- **Strategic Financial Moves:** consider converting a portion of your cryptocurrency to stablecoins to mitigate market volatility. Balance immediate financial gains against potential future growth, and be aware of the tax implications associated with selling your crypto assets. Be mindful of the costs associated with selling cryptocurrencies. Compare fees across different platforms to ensure you retain maximum profits.

- **Planning Your Startup Exit:** develop exit criteria early on and align them with your startup's long-term objectives. This proactive approach allows for a strategic and autonomous exit.

- **Finding the Right Partners:** engage with potential acquisition partners early. Your network can prove invaluable when looking to sell, so active participation in industry events is crucial.

- **Negotiation and Value Alignment:** during M&A negotiations, focus on clauses beyond compensation. Prioritize alignment with the acquiring company's values and culture to ensure a smooth transition.

- **The Importance of Due Diligence:** prepare for the demanding due diligence process, which will scrutinize all aspects of your business. Gathering crucial operational data early on can streamline this phase.

- **Combat Post-Deal Depression (PDD):** recognize the emotional challenges following a business sale and adopt preventative measures like maintaining an abundance mindset and seeking peer support.

- **Post-Exit Strategy:** create a post-exit plan with structured goals to help you navigate the transition. Embrace this period as one of reinvention, self-discovery, and significant personal development.

CONCLUSIONS

Empowering women in
the *Web3* Revolution

The genesis of this book occurred during an Ayahuasca retreat a few years ago, setting off a relentless quest to bring these pages to life. In the whirlwind of my recent years, finding moments for writing was a Herculean task.

Further complicating matters was navigating the labyrinth of the publishing industry to find the right partners who could help me make the vision of this book a reality.

To be honest, it was quite a painful process that cost me a lot of money, sweat, and tears. However, the fact that you are reading these lines is a testament of my perseverance to make this book happen. Is this the perfect vision I had of my book?

Certainly not, but it was the best I could do given the circumstances, and I learned a lot in the process.

Allow me to leave you with this final encouragement: **Dare!** I believe that one of the biggest obstacles for women's success is perfectionism, as highlighted by *"How Women Rise"*. This drive for flawlessness can create a paralyzing fear of risk holding us back from growth and opportunities.

It also creates a comfort zone out of which we rarely navigate, only executing already mastered skills or turning us into eternal students never really applying new knowledge.

Don't be afraid to try. Embrace failure as a stepping stone and you will learn from your mistakes. Yes, you will probably encounter some financial losses in your early investments, and yes, your first startup might fail. For sure, these experiences will hurt but this is growth pain.

I hope you enjoyed this book. My wish is that it helped you get an overview of what *Web3* has to offer, and moreover, that it gave you that little nudge to step out of your comfort zone.

Walking this journey solo can feel overwhelming. In this book I underlined multiple times the importance of community.

So, it would not be fair if I sent you out alone in this journey.

The *Web3* community is here for you, as am I. You can follow me and subscribe to my newsletter on LinkedIn under **https://www.linkedin. com/in/sanjakon/**. Feel free to reach out to me. I am eager to hear about your unique journey.

Finally, don't forget to give back. Advancing even a single step puts you ahead of someone else. Stand by other women who might just need a bit of encouragement to take their first step. If this book was of value to you, sharing it is a simple yet impactful way to assist another woman. Together we can lift each other up and elevate awareness about *Web3*, blockchain, investing, and entrepreneurship among women.

ACKNOWLEDGMENTS

ACKNOWLEDGMENTS

In the spirit of gratitude that this book embodies, I begin my acknowledgments with a heartfelt tribute to my circle of female friends. Elena, Nina, Mia, Maki, Boki, Milica, Clio, Gianna, Margot, Alessandra, Delia, Silvia, Chiara, Sheena, Tania, Giada, Ceci, Mali, and Marti. Your unwavering support and shared wisdom have enriched my life and have been a wellspring of inspiration (for this book). Your friendship has been a constant reminder of the power of unity and the strength found within supportive communities of women.

To Nuno, my esteemed colleague and co-conspirator at Utrust, I owe a profound debt of gratitude. Your vision has broadened my own, inspiring me to reach beyond what I thought possible. In times of doubt, your belief in me and our shared dreams has been an invaluable source of encouragement.

To Peter Diamandis for his mentorship. Through the Abundance 360 mastermind, you have revealed a universe of possibilities to me. Your insights have shone a light on the incredible era in which we live, emphasizing the abundance accessible to all through a shift in perspective.

Turning to my family, my aunt's generosity and kindness have shaped my understanding of boundless giving. Your dedication to others has set a standard of character that I strive to emulate.

I reserve a special acknowledgment for my grandmother, whose teachings on the value of intellectual wealth have profoundly influenced my life. Your wisdom and life lessons have fostered my learning attitude that I now pass on to the world.

This book wouldn't be the same without the sacrifices of my mother, which have laid the foundation of my life's journey.

Your unconditional love has been a constant anchor, offering a safe haven whenever needed. Your presence in my life is an example of the steadfast support that everyone deserves.

Lastly this book is dedicated to Noah. My dear son, may you grow to embrace wisdom, happiness, and the joy in empowering others. I hope you'll find the strength to chase your dreams tirelessly and you'll become a champion of equality.

As I reflect on my journey, I am reminded that our achievements are never ours alone. They are the culmination of the love, guidance, and support bestowed upon us by those who believe in us – our mentors, friends, and family. This book is as much theirs as it is mine.

ABOUT THE AUTHOR

Sanja Kon is a seasoned digital executive, entrepreneur, and influential public speaker renowned for her proven track record in driving sustainable revenue growth across both multinational corporations and pioneering startups within the e-commerce and fintech sectors. Her professional endeavors and speaking engagements are anchored in a steadfast commitment to fostering diversity, inclusion, and ongoing advancement.

A certified business coach and an astute investor in the realms of *Web3* and Life Sciences, Sanja has earned recognition as one of the foremost figures in the crypto sphere, ranking among the top 100 individuals in crypto and top 100 women in *Web3*.

During her tenure as Vice President of Circle Europe, Sanja has wholeheartedly embraced the mission of reshaping global payment paradigms. As the co-founder and CEO of Utrust, she spearheaded the company's successful acquisition by Elrond Network (now MultiversX), strategically positioning it as an influential force in the market.

Driven by an unwavering vision for a future where financial power shifts from traditional institutions to individuals, Sanja champions borderless payments and advocates for financial inclusion as the cornerstone of wealth creation. Renowned as a creative strategist and innovation-centric leader, she has steered multiple triumphant teams, from steering cross-functional groups at PayPal to crafting and executing the European Partnerships strategy at eBay.

Sanja Kon is a highly effective influencer with a talent for assembling and guiding international teams in demanding commercial landscapes. Fluent in multiple languages, her dedication to the potency of communication has led her to share her insights at numerous prestigious international events, addressing diverse audiences on topics spanning women's rights, cryptocurrency, and financial inclusion in the *Web3* era.

Drawing from her early life lessons, where she discovered the perils of complacency, Sanja remains at the forefront of discovering groundbreaking startups and innovative solutions aimed at creating a brighter future. An avid mentor, advisor, and investor, she actively participates in accelerator and incubator programs, nurturing the next generation of trailblazers.

www.ingramcontent.com/pod-product-compliance
Lightning Source LLC
Chambersburg PA
CBHW041158150726
48006CB00016B/2033

* 9 7 9 1 2 8 0 6 2 2 9 5 2 *